veggie-licious

veggie-licious

How to cook with lentils,
chickpeas, beans, tofu and
eat more plant-based foods

Caroline Trickey
Accredited Practising Dietitian • Culinary Nutritionist • Food Lover

'Eat food, not too much, mostly plants.'
Michael Pollan

Contents

Introduction 9

What's in it for you? 10
Fibre
Antioxidants
Inflammation
Phytonutrients
Carbohydrates and Glycaemic Index
Fat
Omega 3 fats
What about protein
How to increase your plant-based intake

Legumes 27

Cooking with legumes 31

Cooking with tofu 45

Cooking with grains 47

Spring & summer 51

Start sprouting in spring 53

It's summer! It's salad time 57

Eating seasonally spring/summer 61

Spring & summer recipes 65

Autumn & winter 159

Roasting vegetables 161

Eating seasonally autumn/winter 163

Autumn & winter recipes 167

Glossary 249

Guide to plant-based protein 256

Pantry staples 260

Meal planning 262

About Caroline Trickey 270

Index 272

Introduction

'Good food prepared from fresh ingredients — ideally seasonal and locally sourced — can and should be at the heart of every happy, healthy family kitchen.'

Hugh Fearnley-Whittingstall

I love food and cooking is my passion.

Hi, I'm Caroline from Healthy Home Cafe. I am a dietitian who sees patients in private practice and I run a cooking school in the Inner West in Sydney, Australia.

In my cooking classes, I combine my knowledge and experience as a dietitian with my background of running a busy café and catering business. My classes are designed to show people how to make delicious, healthy food, and also how to use food as medicine. I love inspiring people and showing them how relatively easy this concept is to apply.

Eating well is vital for me, not only so I can practise what I preach, but also because I recognise that, in all aspects of my life, I feel and perform at my best when supported by a healthy intake.

I am not a vegetarian, but our intake at home is predominantly plant-based. This way of eating is so interesting and varied and, apart from being healthier for us, is also better for our planet.

In Australia we are particularly lucky to have influences from so many different cultures from all over the world and I use this inspiration when preparing our food at home and the recipes for my cooking classes. We eat mostly organic, seasonally based food at home and in my classes.

This book is a selection of my favourite plant-based dips, burgers, soups, salads, mains and more. In it, I have included recipes that have proved the most popular from my cooking classes and website www.healthyhomecafe.com.

I hope you enjoy cooking them as much as I do.

Caroline
Sydney 2017

What's in it for you?

The benefits of a plant-based intake

A whole food, plant-based intake is the healthiest way to eat. A plant-based intake includes all vegetables, fruit, nuts, seeds, legumes and wholegrains — basically anything that is a plant or that grows on a plant.

Eating a plant-based diet is the one commonality that the longest living, healthy populations from around the world have, such as the Okinawans and Cretans.

Plant-based intakes have been shown in thousands of epidemiological (population based) and other accredited studies to
- reduce weight and obesity
- help prevent cancer
- prevent or reverse heart disease
- prevent and improve control in type 2 diabetes
- increase energy and vitality
- improve circulation, sleep and mood
- promote healthy digestion.

Typically this way of eating is based on foods that are minimally processed and if well balanced, a plant-based intake will provide all the macronutrients — carbohydrates, proteins and fats — required by the body for its many metabolic processes. Plant-based foods are also rich in important vitamins, minerals, fibre, antioxidants and phytonutrients, all of which are required for the body to function optimally, and are best sourced from whole foods.

Better for us and better for our planet

We cannot meet the ever-increasing demand for meat (due to increasing populations and nations which, as they become wealthier, aspire to a Western-style, high meat intake) without further damaging our planet. Around the globe, wild habitats have already been demolished, deforestation is destroying important ecosystems and contributing to climate change, and water sources are being depleted or polluted; not to mention greenhouse gas emissions (GHG), antibiotic resistance and the inhumane treatment of some (often intensively-reared) farm animals.

Legume, grain and vegetable crops on the other hand have a much smaller ecological footprint. A plant-based diet requires only one third of the land needed to support a meat and dairy diet. I am not at all suggesting that everyone become vegetarian, but we need to decrease our current intake of meat, especially here in Australia, and eat more plant-based foods.

Fibre

One of the most significant features of plant-based foods is their high fibre content. In fact fibre is only found in plant foods. To be healthy you need to eat more than 30 grams of fibre every day, which means eating a reasonable quantity of plant foods *every* day. Current consumption of less than 20 grams a day means the average Australian does not consume enough fibre.

Fibre keeps the digestive system healthy and prevents constipation. A high-fibre intake can also assist with weight management and appetite control, lower your risk of diabetes, heart disease and certain cancers, reduce inflammation, regulate immune function, reduce reflux and relieve some forms of irritable bowel syndrome.

What is fibre?

Fibre is the indigestible part of edible plant-based foods — fruit, vegetables, nuts, seeds, legumes and whole grains — that your body cannot digest or absorb. Unlike other food components, such as fats, proteins or carbohydrates, which your body is able to break down and absorb, fibre is mostly resistant to these processes. Instead, it passes relatively unchanged through your stomach and small intestine. It then undergoes complete or partial fermentation in the large intestine (bowel or colon) and the remaining portion is then eliminated out of your body in the form of faeces (aka poos or number twos).

There are three different types of fibre. The most well-known are soluble and insoluble fibres. Resistant starch is the third and most recently recognised type of fibre. You need to consume a balance of all three to receive the beneficial effects that each offers.

Soluble fibre dissolves in water to form a gel-like matter which helps to soften the faeces, helping them pass through the gut more easily, keeping you regular. It slows down the digestion and absorption of carbohydrate foods, which helps to keep blood sugar levels steady and can lower LDL cholesterol levels. All plant-based foods contain soluble fibre, but legumes in particular are an excellent source of soluble fibre.

Insoluble fibre adds bulk to faeces and stimulates peristaltic action in the intestines to keep them moving, pushing matter through for elimination. This helps to prevent constipation and associated problems such as diverticulitis and haemorrhoids. Insoluble fibre is found in the skin of all fruit and vegetables as well as in many wholegrains (in particular, wheat) and legumes.

Resistant starch is the part of starchy food (approximately 10 percent) that resists normal digestion in the stomach and small intestine, so it arrives unchanged in the large intestine (bowel). Bacteria that inhabit the large bowel (part of our 'gut microbiome') break down (ferment) and change the resistant starch into short-chain fatty acids (SCFAs) which protect against bowel cancer, play a role in lowering blood cholesterol levels and maintain the pH of the large intestine at a level supportive of the growth of healthy bacteria. You will find resistant starch in legumes, barley, oats and corn as well as cooked and cooled potato, pasta and rice.

Fibre and the gut microbiome

Your gut is home to trillions of bacteria and this just happens to be a very good thing. This diverse community of microbes lives happily with you in a mutually beneficial relationship where they rely on you for food and shelter and you need them for functions critical to your health and wellbeing.

The term microbiota refers to the collection of microorganisms, mainly comprising bacteria, that live in your gut which, along with their DNA, form your microbiome, also referred to as gut flora. They reside mostly in the large intestine.

These bacteria play a key role in digestion and help with the absorption and synthesis of nutrients. They also influence your metabolism, body weight, immune regulation, brain function and mood. Your microbiome is unique to you, like a bacterial fingerprint, and research suggests that a diverse range of gut bacteria is most important for optimal health.

Your gut microbiome begins to develop in very early life and is influenced by birth delivery method, genetics, age, stress, exposure to infection or illness, environment, medication use and diet. In fact, what you eat can quickly change the type of bacteria in your gut.

Good gut health is vital to reduce your risk, or to manage, almost every chronic condition.

Dysbiosis Intestinal dysbiosis is an imbalance in your microbial ecosystem, where pathogenic (bad) bacteria begin to dominate over non-pathogenic or beneficial bacteria. Such changes in gut flora are associated with the development of irritable bowel syndrome (IBS). Dysbiosis can also compromise intestinal permeability, cause a 'leaky gut' and increase susceptibility to inflammatory conditions such as inflammatory bowel diseases (IBD) or bowel cancer, asthma, metabolic syndrome, cardiovascular disease and obesity.

Probiotics A probiotic is a specific strain of bacteria or yeast that promotes health for the host and competes with, thus protects against, disease-causing bacteria. Most of the friendly bacteria that make up your intestinal flora are probiotics. They are also found in some fermented foods like yoghurt, sauerkraut, miso and kimchi.

Prebiotics Prebiotics are high fibre foods that pass through the upper part of your gut undigested and end up as a food source for your beneficial microbes (probiotics), keeping them happy and supporting diversity. Most whole plant foods that contain soluble fibre and all foods with resistant starch are prebiotics. Prebiotic foods include legumes — lentils, dried beans, peas, soy beans and chickpeas, artichokes — globe and Jerusalem, chicory root, bananas, endives, garlic, leeks, onions, parsnips, almonds, honey, unrefined wheat, rye, oats, barley, polenta and corn.

Eating a high fibre intake that includes plenty of colourful plant foods will ensure a richer and more diverse gut microbiome, keeping it and you healthy, balanced and functioning optimally.

Antioxidants

Foods naturally rich in dietary fibre also contain many beneficial antioxidants. In fact, it is very likely that the health benefits from these foods occur, in part, from 'phytonutrients', which are specific types of antioxidants that are closely associated with the fibre components of food.

Antioxidants are biochemical compounds that can protect you from ageing, inflammation, oxidative stress and many chronic diseases. They prevent cellular damage by removing 'free radicals', controlling free radical production and inhibiting other negative oxidation reactions that occur as a part of normal metabolism.

Free radicals are a by-product of normal body cell functions and can also come from outside sources such as pollution, pesticides, drugs, fumes, lead, mercury and radiation, as well as lifestyle factors such as smoking, stress, alcohol, excess sunlight and poor food choices. They don't actually like being 'free' and prefer to latch on to other substances; however, when they do so they can cause damage. When free-radical damage goes unchecked by antioxidants, it can cause significant harm to body cells and tissues which can lead to disease.

Antioxidants are found in all plant-based foods such as fruit, vegetables, legumes, nuts, seeds and whole grains. Antioxidants are also abundant in herbs and spices.

Antioxidants include many vitamins e.g. vitamins C, E, K and beta-carotene, the precursor to vitamin A, minerals e.g. selenium, zinc and copper, and the sub-group phytonutrients.

Inflammation

Research has linked chronic systemic inflammation to almost every major disease. Inflammation is present in auto-immune conditions, is a feature of joint inflammation and arthritis, is indicated in asthma and allergies, accelerates the ageing process, encourages weight gain and can make weight loss more difficult.

Most of us have experienced inflammation in the form of a pimple or rash. It is a natural body reaction to infection and injury. Immune-response signals increase blood flow to get more immune cells and nutrients to the affected site to fight infection and repair the body's cells and tissues. You may notice this as pain, swelling, heat and redness. This type of acute inflammation is a normal and necessary part of the body's defence mechanisms and healing process. It helps protect us against life-threatening situations by eliminating bacteria, viruses, and altered self-cells that could otherwise lead to disease. But sometimes inflammation doesn't end when it is supposed to. Instead, it sticks around in a low-grade, chronic form, silently targeting healthy tissues, causing damage and disease.

Inflammation is fuelled by many factors, including stress, lack of sleep, high blood pressure or sugar levels, abdominal obesity, cigarette smoke and to a large degree, what you eat.

The good news is that a plant-based intake has an anti-inflammatory effect in the human body. Whole plant foods contain powerful antioxidants that interact with, and downregulate, genes that promote inflammation. In fact, a plant-based intake is not only very effective at preventing inflammation, but can also help dampen any active inflammation.

Phytonutrients

The word 'phytonutrient' comes from Greek 'phyto' meaning 'plant', and 'nutrient' meaning 'vital substances for health'. These substances occur naturally only in plants. They are non-essential nutrients, meaning that they are not required by the human body for sustaining life, but they are necessary for optimal health as they provide health benefits way beyond those that essential nutrients can provide. They are a sub-class of antioxidants and it is these natural compounds that give plants their distinctive colour, flavour and smell.

Thousands of different phytonutrients, each with unique disease-preventing properties, have been identified, but there are many more still to be discovered.

Phytonutrients are powerful health-promoting substances to include in your intake. There is growing evidence that they play a crucial role in helping to maintain human health and prevent a number of diseases, such as cardiovascular disease, diabetes, Alzheimer's, macular degeneration and many cancers.

The reported health benefits from phytonutrients are only available when eating plant-based foods, not when supplements are used. Phytonutrients appear to work synergistically with the vitamins, minerals, fibre and other important nutrients found in plants. The crucial interaction of hundreds of different phytonutrients when eating a combination of food appears to be lost when taken in pill form. Not surprisingly, a pill cannot do what eating real, whole food can!

Fruit and vegetables tend to be categorised into five colour groups, according to the phytonutrients they contain. Each colour provides various health benefits and no one colour is superior to another. Typically, the deeper the colour, the more phytonutrients present in the food. Notable exceptions are cauliflower, garlic and onions, which contain plenty of these incredibly healthy substances. Note also that the colour of a food does not necessarily mean it contains only one type of phytonutrient, most plant-based foods contain multiple phytonutrients.

Research suggests that diversity is more important than amount if you want to gain the most benefit from your phytonutrient intake. Different phytonutrients have unique health benefits thanks to their specific chemical structures, but they work best as a team to protect your health. In other words, you need to include fruit and vegetables from each of the colour groups every day (eat the rainbow), to meet your body's needs for all of the different phytonutrients. Good news considering it would be pretty boring if you just ate carrots and broccoli every day!

To maximize your intake of phytonutrients:

- Eat phytonutrient-rich foods frequently throughout the day. This helps keep blood levels of these components constant and ultimately more effective.
- Eat at least five to seven servings a day of vegetables.
- Eat at least two servings a day of fruit.
- Create your meal around vegetables. Fill at least half your plate with different colours.
- Include the skins of the fruit and vegetables – those that are edible of course! The skins often are a concentrated source of phytonutrients.
- Regularly include a wide range of whole grains and legumes in your intake as they also contain phytonutrients.
- By the way, it's okay to cook your vegetables as most phytonutrients are heat-stable.

COLOUR	PHYTONUTRIENT	HEALTH BENEFITS	FOODS
RED	Lycopene	• Helps control high blood pressure. Reduces risk of heart attacks and cancers, especially prostate	• Fresh tomatoes and tomato-based products. Note that cooking tomatoes increases lycopene bioavailability
	Anthocyanins	• Reduces risk of cancer, diabetes and Alzheimer's	• Strawberries, raspberries, red apples, red cabbage
YELLOW AND ORANGE	Beta-carotene (dark orange)	• Converts to vitamin A in body, integral for vision, immune function and healthy skin. Reduces risk of heart disease and cancer	• Carrots, pumpkin, sweet potatoes, mangoes, apricots, peaches
	Bioflavanoids (yellow-orange)	• Help maintain good vision, teeth/bones and healthy skin	• Oranges, grapefruits, lemons, pears
GREEN	Lutein (yellow-green and leafy greens)	• Helps maintain good vision. Reduces risk of cataracts and age-related macular degeneration	• Kale, spinach, leafy greens, lettuce, peas, kiwifruit
	Indoles (cruciferous vegetables)	• Reduces risk of cancers including breast, prostate and bowel cancer	• Broccoli, cabbage, cauliflower, kale, watercress, Brussels sprouts
WHITE AND BROWN	Allicin	• Helps lower high blood pressure and high cholesterol. • Reduces risk of heart attacks and cancer. Also anti-bacterial and anti-viral properties	• Garlic, onions, leeks, spring onions, chives
PURPLE AND BLUE	Anthocyanins	• Reduce risk of cancer, heart disease, diabetes and age-related amnesia	• Blueberries, blackberries, blackcurrants, purple grapes
	Phenolics	• May slow effects of ageing	• Eggplant, plums, prunes, raisins

Carbohydrates and Glycaemic Index

Many plant foods contain carbohydrate. These are legumes, wholegrains, all fruit and starchy vegetables — potato, sweet potato, corn and yams. A few other vegetables contain smaller amounts of carbohydrate — pumpkin, fresh garden peas, parsnip, beetroot and swede — whereas salad, stir fry, green and other coloured vegetables are virtually carbohydrate free. Nuts and seeds also contain relatively little carbohydrate.

Carbohydrate foods mainly break down to glucose (also called 'sugar') during digestion — this glucose is used as fuel by your body and is the preferred fuel source for your brain. Carbohydrate foods that are high in fibre — and in particular soluble fibre — are typically digested more slowly than those foods low in fibre. Foods that are digested slowly to glucose are called low Glycaemic Index (GI) foods and these raise your blood sugar levels after eating, but do so slowly. This is a good thing.

When blood sugar levels rise, your body produces a hormone called insulin which sweeps the sugar into the cells of your body where it is either used for energy or stored as glycogen in your muscle cells and the liver for later use. If sugar levels rise slowly the body is able to match the amount of insulin needed and produce just enough to manage your sugar levels.

High GI foods, on the other hand, are digested to sugar quickly. Large amounts of insulin are produced as your body tries to drop sugar levels just as quickly. This drop can affect your mood, energy levels, focus and drive hunger. High insulin levels in the blood encourage the conversion of sugar into fat for storage, which in turn can encourage weight gain. Eating this way often sets the scene for insulin resistance and increases the risk of developing type 2 diabetes. High insulin levels can also increase the risk of certain (hormone-related) cancers. High GI foods include highly processed and refined foods such as white bread, most biscuits, cakes and sugary cereals. Some less refined or unprocessed, natural foods are also high GI such as short grain white (jasmine) rice, quick oats, watermelon and most potatoes. If eating these foods, it helps to combine them with a low GI food, such as legumes, as this will slow down digestion. Note that all recipes in this book are low GI.

Most plant foods with carbohydrate are high in soluble fibre and low GI, so are slowly digested. These foods therefore provide the perfect fuel for your body and brain. As well as beans, lentils, chickpeas, corn, sweet potato, whole rolled oats, barley and most fruit, there are some low GI minimally processed foods, such as whole grain or sourdough bread, pasta and muesli.

Fat

Most plant-based foods contain little or no fat and no plant food contains cholesterol. They are also low in saturated fat. Saturated fat is associated with: increasing cholesterol levels in the body and heart disease risk; increased risk of insulin resistance; type 2 diabetes and some cancers.

There are some plant foods that are higher in fat, but they contain mostly healthier mono- and polyunsaturated fats which are used and required by the body to stay healthy. These are nuts, seeds, avocado, olives and soy beans. There are a few plant foods high in saturated fat. They are coconut, cocoa butter (extracted from cocoa beans), and palm oil (or palm kernel oil), which is not only high in saturated fat, but is mostly not sustainably sourced, so best avoided.

Soy beans and tofu, walnuts, chia seeds, linseeds and, to a lesser extent, leafy green vegetables and some legumes, including red kidney beans and chickpeas, are all good sources of the essential omega-3 fatty acids which your body cannot produce, but are essential for a healthy heart, brain, joints, vision and even your mood. So it is a good idea to include these foods daily.

Omega 3 fats

Omega 3 fats are essential polyunsaturated fats (PUFA) that your body cannot make, so you must eat foods that contain them. Omega 3 fats are vital for optimal health; they are incorporated into every cell, tissue and organ in your body and have strong anti-inflammatory effects.

There are four main omega 3 fats: DHA (docosahexaenoic acid), EPA (eicosapentaenoic acid), DPA (docosapentaenoic acid) and ALA (alpha-linolenic acid). DHA and EPA are found primarily in oily fish. DPA, along with smaller amounts of EPA and DHA, is found in animal products, such as organic and some free-range eggs, organic chicken and beef and wild fish.

The only truly essential omega 3 fat is ALA, which is derived from plants. With sufficient intake, your body can convert ALA into DHA and EPA. The efficiency at which it does this is determined by genetics, sex, age and dietary composition. Research shows a higher intake of omega 3 fats is beneficial for those with heart disease or a strong family history of heart disease, high triglycerides, inflammatory or auto-immune conditions.

What if you don't eat fish

Eat more plant-based (ALA) omega 3s from such foods as walnuts, linseeds, tofu, Brussels sprouts, cauliflower, kale and kidney beans. If you are after a more therapeutic dose, you may consider taking an algal supplement. To enhance your intake of omega 3s, limit consumption of omega 6 fats like vegetable oils made from corn, sunflower, safflower, soy bean and grapeseed. While we need some omega 6 fats, eating too much limits your body's ability to absorb and use omega 3 fats.

What about protein?

The most common question I get asked about a plant-based intake is whether you can get enough protein. Yes, you definitely can!

Let me start by stating that protein deficiency is rarely a problem in Australia. The average Australian eats roughly twice as much protein as needed, which is only around 50 grams for women and 70 grams for men, a day. In fact in the Western world we have a high prevalence of issues linked to protein excess while insufficient protein intake is unusual. A diet high in protein can actually contribute to health problems including osteoporosis, kidney disease, calcium stones in the urinary tract and some forms of cancer.

What is protein?

Proteins are made from chains of smaller sub-units called amino acids that your body breaks down during digestion. After being digested, these amino acids are absorbed, put back together and used to make new proteins.

There are about 20 different amino acids commonly found in plant and animal proteins. Your body can make some amino acids; however there are nine amino acids, known as 'essential' amino acids, which must come from the food you eat as they cannot be made by your body. For adults, the eight essential amino acids are: leucine, isoleucine, valine, threonine, methionine, phenylalanine, tryptophan and lysine. For children, histidine is also considered to be an essential ninth amino acid.

Role of protein in your body

Proteins are necessary for growth and repair and play an important role in virtually all metabolic processes in your body. Proteins are used to create structural components such as muscles, blood, skin, hair, nails and internal organs. They are required to make hormones, enzymes (needed for metabolic processes) and immune cells. Proteins transport oxygen and nutrients in your blood and cells and regulate water balance.

Don't waste protein as fuel (energy)

Proteins can also provide your body with an alternate source of energy (measured in kilojoules or calories). Generally you use carbohydrate and fat for energy, but when there is excess dietary protein or inadequate dietary fat and carbohydrate, protein is used. Using protein for energy puts a great workload on your body though, which the burning of fat and carbohydrate does not.

When you use protein for fuel, it is a very inefficient process and results in the production of toxic waste that the liver and kidneys must deal with. Excess protein intake has a diuretic effect (causes loss of water) and very high protein diets accelerate calcium loss which, it used to be thought, was pulled from your bones. However new research suggests that this calcium may actually come from your muscles.

Any excess energy in the form of protein, just as with carbohydrates and fat, is converted to fat and stored.

Plant-based protein sources

Plant-based sources of protein include dried beans, split peas, lentils, chickpeas, soy beans, tofu and other products made from soy, as well as nuts and seeds. There are smaller amounts of protein in whole grains and even fruit and vegetables contain a little protein e.g. bananas contain about 2 per cent protein while mushrooms and kale have around 3 per cent.

Plant protein foods compared to animal protein foods:
- are typically lower in saturated fat
- do not contain cholesterol
- do not contain haem iron (haem iron is the most readily absorbed source of iron, but an excess of it is linked to inflammatory conditions such as bowel cancer and heart disease)
- are higher in fibre
- are good sources of antioxidants and phytonutrients
- have anti-inflammatory effects.

This helps to explain why vegetarian intakes are beneficial for many health outcomes including a reduced risk of our three biggest killers — heart disease, type 2 diabetes and cancer.

Note: See table on the following page and also on pages 256–258 for further information about food sources of protein and how to check your protein intake.

How does 'protein combining' work?

Animal protein foods contain large amounts of all the essential amino acids required by your body in a balanced quantity and are referred to as 'complete' proteins.

Most plant protein foods contain all the essential amino acids you require but the amounts of one or two of these amino acids may be low. For example, legumes are low in an amino acid called methionine and many grains are low in lysine.

Because different plant foods are low in different amino acids, but when combined together they make a complete set, they are often called complementary proteins. It was once thought that certain combinations of plant foods, such as legumes with grains, had to be eaten at the same meal for you to get all the essential amino acids. We now know that the body keeps a pool of these indispensable amino acids which can be used to complement dietary proteins so protein combining is not necessary at meal times.

Simply eating a wide variety of plant foods over the day (meaning grains plus legumes plus nuts/ seeds and vegetables) will ensure that your protein needs are easily met. Eating this way will also provide you with an adequate intake of energy and all other nutrients required for optimal health, including iron, zinc, calcium and vitamin B12*.

*Note: Vitamin B12 is usually found in animal products such as eggs, dairy and meat. However it is in nutritional yeast, some fortified soy products and fortified plant milks.

A few plant-based foods are actually high-quality or 'complete' proteins — i.e. they contain large amounts of all essential amino acids. They are soy, quinoa and amaranth.

Many people believe that a high-protein intake leads to increased muscle mass. It is actually the stimulation of muscle tissue through exercise, not eating extra protein, which leads to muscle growth.

NUTRIENT COMPOSITION OF KEY PLANT-BASED FOODS

FOOD PER 100 GRAMS	PROTEIN grams	FAT grams	SATURATED FAT grams	CARBO-HYDRATE grams	FIBRE grams	GLYCAEMIC INDEX
Butter beans, cooked	6.4	0.3	0.1	10.2	5.3	36
Cannellini beans, tinned	6.2	0.6	0.2	12.2	6.4	31
Chickpeas, cooked	6.3	2.1	0.3	13.3	4.7	31
Lentils, cooked	6.8	0.4	0.1	9.5	3.7	29
Red kidney beans, tinned	6.6	0.6	0.1	14.1	6.5	36
Soy beans, cooked	13.5	7.7	1.2	1.4	7.2	14
Split peas, cooked	6.6	0.4	0.3	6.7	3.9	32
Barley, cooked	2.9	0.9	0.4	18.0	3.5	22
Oats, cooked	2.0	1.4	0.2	10.2	1.7	50
Quinoa, cooked	4.4	1.9	0	21.3	2.8	53
Kale, raw	3.3	0.7	0.1	10.0	2.0	—
Sweet potato, boiled	2.0	0.1	0	15.2	3.2	44
Tofu	12.0	7.3	1.0	0	7.0	—
Almonds	19.5	54.7	4.0	4.0	8.8	—
Pumpkin seeds	30.2	49.1	8.7	10.7	6.0	—

— means the food has insufficient carbohydrate to measure the Glycaemic Index or the food has not yet been analysed

How to increase your plant-based intake

PROTEIN FOODS

Fill a quarter of the plate with a wide variety of protein rich foods such as legumes*, tofu, eggs, nuts, seeds or dairy.

NON-STARCHY VEGETABLES OR SALAD

Fill at least half the plate with non-starchy vegetables (any vegetable except potato, sweet potato or corn) or salad. They contain loads of nutrients — the vitamins, minerals, antioxidants and phytonutrients your body needs to help you look and feel your best. The greater the variety and colour, the better!

LOW GI CARBOHYDRATES

Fill a quarter of the plate with low GI carbohydrate foods such as sweet potato, corn, Nicola or Carisma (low GI) potatoes, legumes*, grains like quinoa or barley, long grain brown rice or a wholemeal pasta.

AND ...

include in your meal some healthy fat (such as extra virgin olive oil, avocado, nuts and seeds) to help you absorb all the fat soluble vitamins and phytonutrients in the meal.

*Legumes, which consist of lentils, chickpeas, split peas and dried beans, appear in both the protein and carbohydrate sections in the above plate. That is because they are both a great source of protein and an excellent low GI carbohydrate food.

Legumes

In Australia we are finally starting to embrace the humble legume, which is just wonderful to see. They now feature on most restaurant menus and many different options are readily available in supermarkets. Of course I'm not at all surprised as I love legumes, and let's face it, there is a lot to love about them. They are cheap, filling, easy to use, very versatile and very, very nutritious.

Mind you, many parts of the world have been singing their culinary praises for years. They are used extensively throughout India and I'm sure you are familiar with dhal; the French have cassoulet; the Lebanese love their hommus and Moroccans their harira, the chickpea and lamb soup. My favourite Greek dishes include the delicious lentil soup 'Fakes', split pea dip 'Fava' and 'Gigantes', their version of giant baked beans; and don't forget Mexico where a meal isn't complete without beans, usually the black ones.

Yet in Australia, so many of us were brought up eating meat and three veg, and for such a long time legumes have been shunned as food only to be eaten by peace-loving hippies.

Perhaps it's because in their dry state, they do not immediately strike you as appetising, or that most people are unfamiliar with how to cook with them? Perhaps it's because their first experience was of something with a mushy texture that gave them wind! But they are, as you will find out if you make any of the recipes in this book, delicious. Plus, they are very easy to use – lentils as they are quick to cook; tinned beans or tinned chickpeas, as they are ready to use; by using a pressure cooker, as this significantly cuts down the cooking time.

Also called pulses, legumes are the seeds from plants whose fruit is enclosed in a pod. They are better known to us as different varieties of dried beans, which includes baked beans (navy beans), soy beans, split peas, lentils and chickpeas. They can be used to add body, texture and a certain robustness to everything from dips, soups and salads, to tagines, stews and curries. They can even be used as a flour replacement in sweet baking. Check out the recipes for 'Apple cake' with chickpeas on page 245 and 'Black bean brownie' on page 246.

Certain legumes lend themselves to different gastronomic masterpieces. Some, like butter beans, are quite creamy, others such as adzuki beans are nutty, kidney beans are meaty and brown lentils are quite earthy. Some hold their shape where others, like split peas and split red lentils, 'melt' and slip silently into sauces, soups and casseroles.

Legumes are dormant nutritional powerhouses that, in their dry form, can stay in your cupboard for months on end. But I do not suggest that you leave them untouched for long as the older they are, the longer they take to cook. I like to buy small amounts as needed from a shop with a high turnover, and use them promptly. When required, simply soak your beans and chickpeas (if cooking lentils, they do not need to be soaked) to revive them and bring them 'back' to life. They are usually then cooked for their precise time and eaten. However, they can also be left to sprout,

and in this form can be eaten raw in all manner of ways, which I love to do in spring and summer. See *Start sprouting in spring* on pages 53–55 for how to sprout legumes.

Dried legumes are very cheap and they almost triple in volume when cooked. They also have the added benefit that when cooking from scratch, you can cook them to the texture you want, depending on the dish you need them for. If using in a salad they need to be firmer, but for a dip or burger a softer texture is preferable.

Of course, tinned legumes are perfect for when you are short on time as they need no preparation. Just drain and rinse and they are ready to use. They are fabulous when you need a meal, salad or dip in minutes, or need to extend a casserole or curry to feed more hungry mouths. You should keep a good stash of the different types in your cupboard at all times so you are ready should any of these situations arise. Of course, if you have just a little extra time you can always opt for lentils, which do not require soaking, and cook within just 20 minutes.

> Legumes …. 'the Sleeping Beauties of the
> kitchen cupboard, awaiting your culinary kiss of life.'
> Hugh Fernleigh Whittingstall

When it comes to nutrition, it's hard to beat legumes as they are one of the most nutritious foods available. In particular, they are:

- A valuable source of protein. Half a cup of cooked legumes contains around 7 grams of protein (for more on protein and requirements refer to pages 256–258).

- High in fibre to keep your digestive system and bowels healthy and reduce your risk of bowel cancer. Half a cup of cooked legumes contains between 4 and 7 grams of fibre (we need in excess of 30 grams a day).

- A good source of soluble fibre which can help to lower LDL cholesterol levels and reduce your cardiovascular risk.

- A low GI source of carbohydrate. This means they will keep you full for longer and provide a sustainable source of energy. This also makes them an excellent food to help prevent and manage diabetes.

- An important source of B-group vitamins, which are your energy vitamins (including folate, essential for women of child-bearing age).

- A source of the minerals iron, zinc, magnesium and calcium.

- An excellent source of phytonutrients (powerful plant antioxidants).

- A very small but relevant source of essential omega-3 fatty acids.

- Low in saturated fat.

- Low in calories or kilojoules.

Cooking with legumes

Lentils

Lentils are the easiest of all the legumes to cook with. In my cooking classes, I suggest beginners start with lentils as their first legume for three reasons. Firstly they do not require soaking, unlike dried beans and chickpeas. Secondly, they are quick to cook. Finally, with their neutral flavour, they take on the flavour of whatever they are cooked in, from onion and stock to soups and casseroles.

Types of lentils

The most popular types of lentils available in Australia are:
- Red lentils — either whole or split
- Brown, also known as Green lentils
- Puy lentils also called French green lentils
- Black Beluga lentils

Red lentils

Red lentils are the most common type of lentil and are sold predominantly as split lentils. They are a salmon-pink colour when dry, but turn golden when cooked. These lentils are very mild in flavour so they tend to take on the flavour of what they are cooked in. Since they cook within 6–10 minutes, they are the fastest to cook of all the lentils. Best in purées, dips, patties or soups as they are quite 'mushy' when cooked. They are also a great gluten free, high-fibre way to thicken gravies, stews, casseroles and curries.

Recipes to try
- *Pumpkin and red lentil soup*
- *Quick lentil curry*

Brown/green lentils

These are the only type of lentils you can buy pre-cooked in tins, but are also easy to find in dry form. They take around 20 minutes to cook and have a slight earthy flavour which I enjoy.

Recipes to try
- *Lemony lentil soup*
- *Lentil burgers with cashews*
- *Lentil Bolognese*

Puy lentils or French green lentils

Small slate-green lentils, delicate with a slightly peppery flavour, Puy lentils hold their shape well when cooked, which takes around 20 minutes and make a delicious side dish or bed for meat, chicken or fish, prepared simply with just olive oil, fresh parsley or thyme, salt and pepper. Their name comes from the Le Puy region where they were originally grown in France; however they are also now grown in Australia. Those grown in Australia are not allowed to use the Puy name, so are called French green lentils.

Recipes to try
- *Lentil Bolognese*

Black Beluga lentils

These are one of the smallest in the lentil family. Shiny black in colour, they are super easy to cook taking only 15 to 20 minutes of boiling. They look like caviar (hence the name), so they make an interesting garnish on top of canapés, but are also great in soups and salads.

Recipes to try
- *Black Beluga lentil salad with baby kale, pumpkin and beetroot*

• • •

Lentils cook more slowly if they're combined with salt or acidic ingredients such as tomatoes or lemon juice, so add these last. Also it's wise to remember that older lentils take longer to cook.

Red and brown lentils are easily available in all supermarkets and Indian grocery stores. Puy or French green lentils are available in some supermarkets, but also in many greengrocers and health food stores, along with black Beluga lentils.

To cook dried lentils
1. Rinse first, then place in a large pot and cover with at least three times the volume of water.
2. Place a lid on the pot and bring to the boil over high heat.
3. Turn heat down to a simmer and cook, half-covered for 10-20 minutes, depending on the type of lentil, how old they are and how well you like them cooked.

Split peas

Split peas could be easily mistaken for lentils as they look very similar. However, they come from a different species of plant. They are also different from fresh garden peas, which are in season in spring and available all year round frozen.

'Field peas', as the variety of split peas is called, are grown specifically to be dried as they are too tough to be eaten fresh. After harvesting they are podded, skinned and dried, and then usually split naturally or are mechanically split. The splitting process increases the surface area, so reduces cooking time.

Available as yellow or green, split peas are probably most well-known from their inclusion in pea (and ham) soup, where either colour can be used; the yellow ones, sometimes called chana dhal (dal), are used to make dhal in many countries and fava dip in Greece. The two colours are the same nutritionally, but green peas are slightly sweeter than the yellow, milder flavoured ones.

Like lentils, they do not need to be soaked before cooking; however as they take a lot longer to cook than lentils (approx. 50 minutes), many people prefer to pre-soak them to cut down the cooking time.

To cook split peas

1. Place in a colander and rinse, then transfer to a large saucepan and cover with at least triple the amount of cold water. Place a lid on the pot and bring to the boil over high heat.
2. Turn heat down to a simmer and cook, half-covered for 50–60 minutes.
3. Pre-soaked peas (soaked overnight) will take 30–40 minutes to cook.
4. In a pressure cooker, split peas will take about 15 minutes, pre-soaked peas take about 10 minutes.

Note: do not add salt when cooking split peas, as this slows down the cooking process.

Recipes to try

- Use yellow split peas in place of all of the red lentils in the red lentil dhal recipe, or use $1/2$ split peas and $1/2$ red lentils. With either adaptation, increase the cooking time to 50–60 minutes and you may need to add a little extra water.

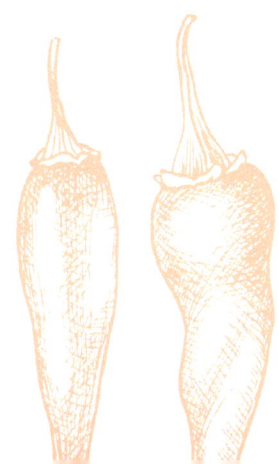

Chickpeas

I love the spherical shape of chickpeas, their firm but soft texture and mild flavour which lend themselves to all sorts of interesting dishes and cuisines. In tinned form, they are my go-to legume when I am in a hurry.

Chickpeas are an amazingly versatile addition to a wide variety of dishes; everything from soups, dips and salads to curries and tagines. They are also the main ingredient in falafels, the deliciously tasty Lebanese deep-fried balls. Besan flour, which is made by grinding chickpeas, can be used in baked goods, vegetable fritters and makes a great flatbread which can be used as a pizza base (see my recipe for Socca).

How to find chickpeas

Chickpeas are sold pre-cooked in tins or in dried form.

Tinned chickpeas are very convenient and require only to be drained, rinsed quickly under cool running water and they are ready to use. If being used to make a dip or in a salad, they don't need to be heated, but sometimes I like to 'toast' them in a pan with some olive oil and spices first. For other recipes such as soups or stews, add them at the end and cook just long enough to heat them through (2–3 minutes).

Dried chickpeas need to be soaked overnight and then cooked so that they soften up. Home-cooked chickpeas are more flavoursome than tinned, come at a fraction of the cost, and can be cooked to your desired texture such as firm or soft. Here's my rule of thumb: one cup of dry chickpeas yields three cups when cooked (which is equal to a little more than two 400 gram tins).

Tinned chickpeas are always worthwhile to have in your kitchen cupboard. They can be stored indefinitely if it's cool. Dried chickpeas should be stored in an air-tight container at cool room temperature. It is best to use them within 6 months because as they get older, they take longer to cook.

Leftover cooked chickpeas will keep for 3 to 4 days in the refrigerator, stored in an air-tight container. They can also be frozen although they can sometimes end up being a bit mushy when thawed, so plan to use them in dishes like dips and soups that do not require firm, whole chickpeas.

To cook dried chickpeas

1. Place the chickpeas in a large bowl. Cover with at least triple the amount of cold water, cover and set aside overnight to soak.
2. The next day, drain well, rinse then transfer to a saucepan or large pot. Cover with fresh water, bring to the boil, then reduce heat to a simmer and cook until tender, approximately 40 minutes to one hour. Or you can cook them using a pressure cooker (after a pre-soak overnight) and they take about 18 minutes.
3. Add salt after cooking.

Varieties of chickpeas

There are two main types of chickpeas — Desi and Kabuli, distinguished mainly by seed size, shape and colour:

Desi types are smaller and range in colour from brown, light brown, fawn, yellow, orange, black or green. They are normally de-hulled and split to make dhal and are favoured in India. My local Indian grocery store stocks the whole brown desi (called Tyson) chickpeas which I love to use.

Kabuli types are larger. They are white to cream in colour and are almost exclusively used whole. They are preferred throughout the Mediterranean region and the ones most readily available in Australia.

Recipes to try
- *Falafels*
- *Socca*
- *Pumpkin and chickpea curry*
- *Baked eggplant with chickpeas and green chilli*
- *Green goddess slaw with chickpeas*
- *Peanut butter and chickpea energy balls*

Beans

There are so many different varieties of beans, from adzuki to kidney to mung, with all their glorious colours and shapes. Most come either pre-cooked in tins or are available in dried form:

Tinned beans are already cooked so they only need to be drained and rinsed before using them. This also removes most of the sodium (salt) if they are tinned in brine.

Dried beans except adzuki, black eyed peas and mung beans need to be soaked overnight before you cook them.

You can cook them on the stove in a pot, but I prefer to use a pressure cooker as it is much faster. If you are going to cook beans regularly, I highly recommend investing in a good pressure cooker.

How to cook dried beans

Start by soaking them. Cover with at least triple the amount of cold water, cover and set aside overnight (at least 8 hours). The next day, drain well, rinse then transfer to a saucepan or large pot.

In a pot: Put the pre-soaked and drained beans into your pot and cover with cold water. Bring to a steady boil and don't salt the water as this makes the beans tough. Skim off any sediment as it rises to the surface. Partially cover and cook until tender, topping up with boiling water from the kettle as needed, then drain. See cooking times on page 43. Note that cooking times do vary as older beans take longer to cook.

Dried beans are nutritious, as are all legumes and pulses. They are rich in fibre and are a good source of protein for vegetarians and vegans. Enjoy them as a protein food or as a starchy carbohydrate to help you feel full.

In a pressure cooker: Drain soaked beans, put in pressure cooker and just cover with water. Place lid on securely and bring up to pressure with high heat, then turn heat down to simmer for times as listed on page 43. Natural release allows the pressure cooker to come down to room temperature naturally, fast release is when you place the sealed pressure cooker under cold water to cool it down faster.

If you do not have time to soak beans overnight, try my alternate 'quick soak' method:
- Bring a large pot of water to the boil, add beans, and allow the water to come back to boiling.
- Turn off heat, cover and stand for one hour, then drain, rinse and cook for time as listed on page 43.

Types of beans

There are many types of beans to choose from, and each has its own distinct flavour and texture. The following list includes the most popular varieties and ones that I regularly use and love:

Red kidney beans

Perhaps the most popular, kidney beans have a deep red colour and a lovely slightly sweet flavour. They hold their shape well when cooked, making them a great choice for vegetable stews, chilli, soups and bean salads.

Recipes to try
- *Minestrone*
- *Mushroom and bean burgers*
- use in place of black beans in *Black bean chilli*
- puree them to make 'refried beans' for *Coconut chapati and bean salad stacks*

Black beans

One of my favourites, black beans are also known as turtle beans. They have a very mild, slightly sweet taste. Because of their dense texture, they are perfect when combined with spicy flavours and hot seasonings. They are delicious in chillies and thick soups but also great in salads. Surprisingly they can also be used for sweet dishes like brownies and chocolate cake.

Recipes to try
- *Black bean enchiladas with kale and guacamole*
- *Black bean chilli on soft polenta*
- *Black bean and quinoa burgers*
- *Black bean brownies*

Cannellini beans

Looking like a white version of a kidney bean, cannellini beans are the favourite of the Italians, especially the Tuscans who use them in virtually everything — soups, salads, pasta dishes etc. They are a mild, slightly nutty tasting bean with a fluffy texture.

Recipe to try
- *Creamy cannellini bean and kale soup*
- *White bean dip with garlic and herbs*

Lima (also known as butter) beans

Large creamy white beans that have a buttery, starchy texture and a delicate flavour, Lima beans are great mashed as an alternative to mashed potato, or made into dips or spreads. They are also fabulous in soups and salads, stews or casseroles.

Recipes to try
- Use them in place of the cannellini beans in *Creamy cannellini bean and kale soup*
- *Creamy potato salad with butter beans and mint*

Borlotti beans

A variety of kidney bean, borlotti beans are easily recognised by their marbled appearance of an off-white bean with pretty red-brown streaks. They have a mild, nutty flavour with a smooth creamy texture. These beans are loved by the Italians who use them in soups, salads and casseroles.

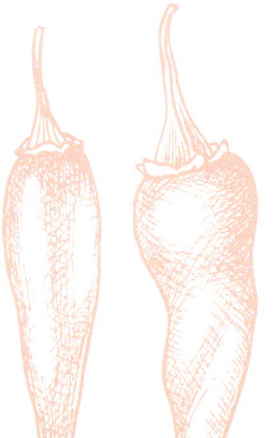

TYPE OF LEGUME	COMMON USES
Adzuki beans, also known as aduki, field peas or red beans	Burgers, soups, stews, sweet bean paste, Japanese and Chinese dishes
Black beans, also known as turtle beans	Burgers, soups, stews or casseroles, rice dishes and Latin American dishes
Black-eyed peas, also known as cowpeas	Salads, casseroles and Southern dishes
Borlotti beans	Soups (especially minestrone), salads and casseroles
Cannellini beans	Dips, burgers, salads, soups, casseroles, pasta dishes
Chickpeas, also known as garbanzo beans	Hommus, burgers or falafel, salads, soups, casseroles, Spanish and Indian dishes
Edamame, also known as green soy beans	Snacks, salads, stir fries, casseroles and rice dishes
Fava beans, also known as broad beans	Dips, stews and side dishes
Lentils	Dips, salads, burgers, casseroles, stews, side dishes, dhal and other Indian dishes
Lima beans, also known as butter or Madagascar beans	Dips, salads, soups and casseroles
Mung beans	Sprouted (bean sprouts), soups, dhal, casseroles
Red kidney beans	Dips, salads (especially as part of 4 bean mix), soups, stews or casseroles, chilli and rice dishes
Roasted soy beans or roasted chickpeas 'chic-nuts'	Snack or garnish for soups and salads
Split peas	Soups, dhal, fava dip

Adzuki beans

These are small browny-red beans and seem to be easier to digest than some of the larger varieties. They do not have to be soaked before cooking and have a less beany-tasting flavour that is a delicious mix of sweet and nutty. They are most well known as the red bean filling in Chinese desserts.

Recipes to try
- Use them in place of kidney beans in *Mushroom and bean burgers*
- *Eggplant and adzuki bean burgers*

Black-eyed peas

Gorgeous cream-coloured beans, despite being called a pea, with a black spot or 'eye'. A great all-rounder as they are terrific in salads, soups and casseroles. They are a favourite as they also do not require soaking before cooking.

Recipes to try
- *Black-eyed peas with garlic and lemon*

Mung beans

Better known in their sprouted form, mung beans are nonetheless fantastic in soups, curries and dhals. They do not need soaking and cook within 20–30 minutes. They are also not as 'wind forming' as some of the larger beans, so are preferable to use if you have a sensitive tummy.

Recipe to try
- Can be used in Dhal.

Soy beans

Soy beans can sometimes be found dried, but I prefer to use the fresh variety – edamame. Available in the freezer section in Asian food stores and also many supermarkets.

Cooking beans

I have included a reference guide on the following page which includes cooking times for all the different legumes.

How much will I get?

- $1/2$ cup of dry beans typically makes around $1 1/3$ cups or 240 grams when cooked. Approximately what you get from one 400 gram tin, which is handy!
- Cooked beans can be kept in the fridge for 3–4 days or frozen for up to 3 months. I like to cook large batches of beans and store them in $1 1/3$ cup, 240 gram portions (the equivalent to a 400 gram tin) in the freezer for quick use.

LEGUME COOKING GUIDE

	Soak overnight	Cook on stove	Cook in pressure cooker — natural release	Cook in pressure cooker — fast release
Red kidney	YES	45–60 minutes	5 minutes	10 minutes
Borlotti beans	YES	45–60 minutes	7 minutes	12 minutes
Black beans	YES	40–50 minutes	3 minutes	5 minutes
Cannellini beans	YES	45–60 minutes	6 minutes	9 minutes
Lima/butter beans	YES	30–40 minutes	1–3 minutes	4 minutes
Adzuki beans	NO	30–40 minutes	2 minutes	5 minutes
Black-eyed peas	NO	45–60 minutes	5 minutes	7 minutes
Mung beans	NO	20–30 minutes	NO	NO
Chickpeas	YES	40–60 minutes	18 minutes	22 minutes
Split peas – yellow or green	NO	50–60 minutes	15–20 minutes	25–30 minutes
Lentils – brown, French green, black Beluga	NO	15–20 minutes	6–8 minutes	8–12 minutes
Lentils – red split	NO	10–15 minutes	NO	NO

This table is a guide only. Beans, chickpeas, and to a lesser degree lentils, vary greatly with cooking time depending on how old they are. It is best to buy small amounts from a shop with a high turnover and use them promptly to prevent the issue of old dried beans that take 'forever' to cook.

If beans are hard for you to digest (because they cause an excess of wind, gas or bloating), start with smaller legumes first like lentils, mung or adzuki beans, and start with a small amount, like ¼ to ⅓ of a cup when cooked, and cook them until they are very soft. Increase the amount slowly (over several weeks) and as time goes by your body will get used to them. When you feel you can digest the smaller beans and lentils easily, move up to the medium sized ones like black beans, then finally try chickpeas and kidney beans.

Cooking with tofu

Tofu, a well-known ingredient in Asian cooking, is a protein-rich food made from soy beans. The soy beans are first cooked and the creamy-white soy liquid (milk) is extracted. Then, similar to the way cheese is made, a curdling agent such as the mineral magnesium carbonate or lemon juice is added. The resulting curd is then compressed into tofu, while the whey is separated off. How firm the tofu is depends on the amount of 'whey' pressed out.

You can make it yourself, however I prefer to leave it to the experts. Also, tofu is easily available and quite cheap to buy, especially in Asian shops where it is cheapest and you will get the biggest variety, as well as in supermarkets and health food stores.

Tofu is relatively flavourless, so it is best in dishes with sauces or gravies like curries, casseroles and soups where it can soak up their flavours. You can also marinade it or serve with a tasty sauce (like satay sauce). Softer varieties are a great replacement for cream cheese in dips and cream in desserts and mousses.

For me, since it is bland in flavour, tofu is all about the texture. I avoid using extra firm tofu as I find it rubbery, yet some of my clients prefer this texture.

Firm tofu holds its shape well but is not as chewy as extra firm. I like to use this for savoury dishes like curries, casseroles and stir fries. As it is a bit drier, firm tofu soaks up flavours very well. Silken firm or pressed tofu is a favourite of mine as it has a firm custard-like texture and it can be used in savoury or sweet dishes. You can marinate it, then bake it and serve it on top of your dish. Be careful if adding it to stir fries and other dishes where it is stirred through, as it breaks apart easily and ends up looking like scrambled eggs (but will taste fine). I also like to use this in firmer textured desserts.

Silken tofu is my absolute favourite tofu as I adore its creamy, custard-like texture which is great in desserts like lemon, mango or chocolate mousse. See recipe on page 149. Yum!

Here are two of my favourite super-quick and easy meals made using tofu:

Baked tofu

- Marinate silken firm tofu in soy sauce or tamari, honey, garlic and ginger for at least 30 minutes or overnight. Remove from marinade, place on baking tray and bake in a hot oven for 10 minutes.
- Serve on top of steamed or stir-fried vegetables with quinoa, barley or brown rice.

Pan-fried tofu cubes

- Heat a large pan over medium heat. When hot, add some extra virgin olive oil and cubes of firm tofu. Cook, turning only a few times until they start to brown on the outside.
- Add some soy sauce or tamari, garlic, sesame oil and water and stir to coat (you can also add a little fresh chilli or sweet chilli sauce).
- Serve on veggies or rice (as suggested above), sprinkle with toasted sesame seeds and garnish with fresh coriander. Mmmm, yum!

Cooking with grains

Too many of us get our grains from just one type — wheat. Often this wheat has been heavily refined and processed and looks nothing like the wheat berries that originally came from the plant. Nutrition-wise, it is a very poor version. The second most consumed grain in Australia is rice — largely as refined white rice — which is also lacking in nutrients and merely provides a dense form of carbohydrate. One of the benefits of learning how to include more plant-based foods in your intake is discovering how to cook other nutritious grains that can replace wheat and rice, and there are heaps to choose from. Here are the ones I like to use:

Barley

Mostly available as pearl barley (polished to remove the hull and some of the outer bran layer, so technically not a wholegrain, but pretty close), this is an amazingly nutritious and very low GI grain (GI is a low 22). Great in soups, salads and risottos, pearl barley also makes an excellent side dish in place of, or mixed with, rice, especially for those with diabetes. It takes anywhere from 25 to 50 minutes to cook. Like legumes, the older it is, the longer it takes to cook.

Buckwheat

Although it has wheat in its name, buckwheat has no relationship to wheat whatsoever. It is a great high-fibre gluten free grain, and delicious in dishes such as pilafs, risottos and salads as well as muesli. I like to toast it quickly first before I cook it in stock or water for 15 minutes.

Cornmeal (or polenta)

Basically, polenta is dried, ground corn — and I love it! It comes in different grades from coarse through to fine, which alters its cooking time (coarse takes longer). It can be used to make soft polenta (see page 225) which is a great replacement for mashed potato, or polenta squares by setting it in a tray and allowing it to cool (refer to my blog for that recipe). Cut into squares and heat in a pan with a drizzle of oil until brown and crisp on the outside or bake in the oven and serve alongside any meal. Mmmm, delicious!

Freekeh

Freekeh is a wheat grain which is picked young while still green, then roasted. It is low GI (GI of 43), high in fibre and higher in protein than most other grains. It can be used in place of rice, cous cous and other grains in salads, pilafs or as a side dish to stir fries, casseroles or curries. It takes around 45 minutes to cook.

Rice — wild and brown

Try wild rice — nutrient-rich, can be cooked and mixed through regular rice, or use brown rice, which is less refined. Long grain and Basmati rice are lower GI.

Oats

Oats are one of my favourite grains. Traditionally used to make porridge and muesli, I love using oats in cakes, biscuits, slices, energy balls and in place of breadcrumbs in veggie and meat burgers. Whole rolled oats are lower GI, so very filling, but the finely chopped quick cooking oats are medium-high GI. Oats are high in fibre and contain a special type of soluble fibre that has been shown to help reduce LDL cholesterol levels. They are easy to digest for most people and I think including them for breakfast is the best way to start the day!

Quinoa

Quinoa is a highly nutritious seed that we use like a grain. It makes a terrific base for salads or side dishes in place of rice. Quinoa is high in magnesium and a good source of iron and many other essential minerals, plus it has the highest protein content of any grain. Available in white, red or black varieties, it has a mellow flavour (white has the least flavour), is gluten free and easy to digest. Choose Australian grown wherever possible. The easiest way to cook quinoa is to rinse first then boil in water for 12–20 minutes (note that black quinoa takes approximately 5 minutes longer to cook than white or red). However like buckwheat, you can also toast it first.

Millet

Often known only because of its inclusion in birdfeed, millet is an incredibly nutritious tiny round yellow-coloured grain. Popular due to it being gluten free, millet is available either hulled, puffed or as flour.

Hulled millet can be used to make porridge, in salads, burgers or as a side-dish in place of rice, cous cous, polenta or mashed potatoes. The easiest way to cook millet is in boiling water or stock for 20–25 minutes. It can also be lightly toasted first in a dry pan before cooking. Puffed millet is often added to gluten free cereals and the flour is traditionally used to make flatbreads, dosa or roti in Africa and India.

Spelt

Spelt is an ancient variety of wheat. It has become very popular as people who have trouble digesting wheat and have issues with bloating, wind and other irritable bowel-like symptoms, can often better tolerate spelt. This is because spelt is low in wheat fructans (which are a type of FODMAP). Spelt flour is available in most supermarkets and you can buy spelt berries in many health food stores. Many artisan sourdough bakeries make spelt bread and spelt pasta is available from most supermarkets, delis and gourmet food stores. Spelt flour is typically less refined than regular wheat flour making it lower GI, however do choose the wholemeal one. You can use spelt flour anywhere you use wheat flour, so in breads, cakes, biscuits etc. Spelt berries can be used to make salads, risotto, in soup, as a side dish in place of rice or even as a dessert, cooked in apple juice with raisins and cinnamon and topped with yoghurt and walnuts. Yum! Spelt berries take 25–40 minutes to cook, depending on how old they are.

- For recipe ideas using grains go to www.healthyhomecafe.com

spring & summer

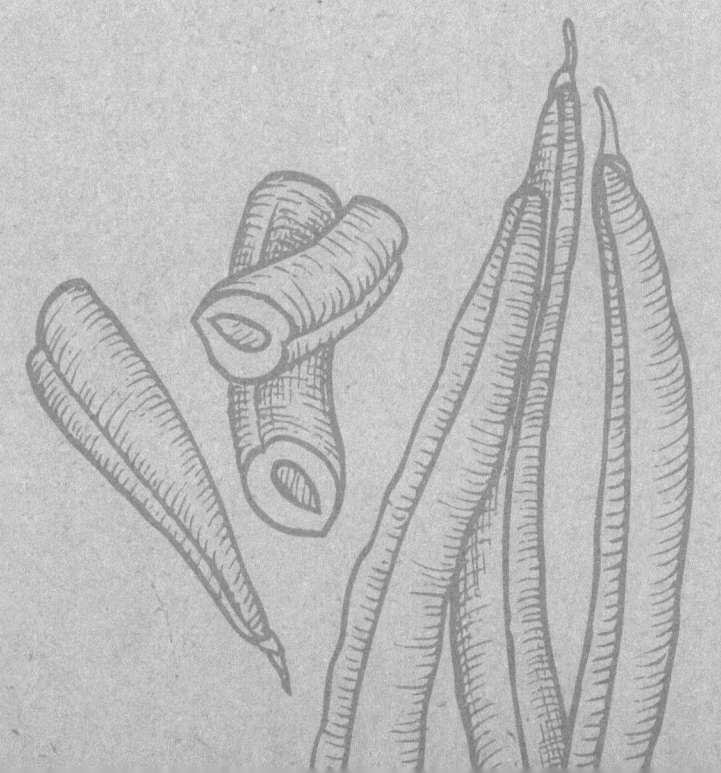

Start sprouting in spring

If sprouts just mean alfalfa and (mung) bean sprouts to you, then you are in for a great delight when you discover that there are many more options well worth trying. Most seeds, grains, beans, chickpeas and lentils can easily be sprouted, and you will now find many of these sprouts readily available in fruit and vegetable stores as well as supermarkets. Each has its own unique flavour, they are incredibly versatile and very nutritious.

Sprouting is really quick and easy to do yourself. It only requires basic equipment, doesn't take up much room and is very economical (most seeds yield in excess of four times their starting volume). Nothing is as satisfying and wondrous as when you get to watch your static lentils, beans, chickpeas and grains suddenly transform when they sprout and become a vibrant, living food source in just a few days.

What is sprouting?

Lentils, chickpeas, beans and grains are seeds, meaning they are nutritional powerhouses with the potential to grow into a plant. Sprouting is the germination process when a seed starts its conversion into a plant and develops a tail-like protrusion, but growth is arrested within just a few days. All you need to do to activate this growth is soak them in water.

The method is exactly the same for whole grains, seeds, lentils, chickpeas and beans —only the time required for both soaking and germination varies (see table on next page).

Why sprout?

There are two great reasons to DIY sprouts:
1. Sprouts are a living, enzyme-rich food that are easy to digest, packed with plant protein and essential vitamins.
2. Sprouting is one of the simplest and cheapest ways to provide yourself with this incredible home-grown nutrient-dense food source in your own kitchen.

As the seed becomes a seedling, carbohydrate is used for growth, and the nutrient profile, as well as antioxidant content, increases. For example:
- protein content increases by 15–30 percent and long chain proteins are split into smaller, more easily digested molecules
- fibre increases
- B vitamins like niacin and riboflavin increase, as do vitamin C, beta-carotene, vitamins E, K, calcium, phosphorus and to a lesser extent, iron

Sprouting also enhances the bioavailability of certain nutrients, meaning these nutrients may be more easily absorbed, including zinc, iron and calcium.

For those who suffer from gas and digestive discomfort from cooked legumes and grains, sprouting helps break down some of the carbohydrate chains that ferment to create intestinal gas, so sprouted legumes and grains are more easily tolerated. Due to this impressive transformation as well as the powerful combination of increased bioavailability, nutrient density, phytonutrient and antioxidant content, sprouts are a valuable addition to your intake.

Ways to use sprouted grains, seeds, nuts, and legumes

- As a snack. Mix sprouts with some spices and a little extra virgin olive oil
- In or as a salad (for example, sprouted quinoa tabbouleh, and see 'Sprouted spring salad' on page 134)
- On top of salads or other foods as an edible garnish
- In dips and spreads. For example, try a sprouted chickpea hommus or a sprouted sunflower seed spread
- In soups, curries, stews, burgers and stir fries.

What to sprout

Most seeds and grains sprout easily, as do many legumes. Nuts are more difficult to sprout.

SPROUTING GUIDELINES

FOOD	SOAKING TIME (hours)	SPROUTING TIME (days)
Alfalfa	8–12	3–4
Buckwheat	6	2–3
Chickpeas	8	2–4
Lentils	8	2–4
Millet	5	12 hours
Mung beans	8–12	2–4
Radish	8–12	3–5
Sunflower seeds	8	3–5
Quinoa	4	2–3
Wheat berries	7	2–4
Wild rice	9	3–5

When to sprout

Sprouts can be grown all year round, but I prefer to do this in Spring and Summer. The temperature in Sydney at this time seems to be best for germination of most seeds, plus energetically it feels like the right time of year to be producing and eating raw foods like sprouts.

Basic sprouting guidelines

Pick over and remove any seeds that are damaged, split or just don't look quite right. Rinse then place in a bowl and cover with plenty of water. Set aside to soak as per chart below. Usually it is overnight or for 8–10 hours. The next day, drain and rinse twice before transferring to your clean sprouting jar or container. Cover securely with the muslin cloth or other breathable top.

Place jar in a dark cupboard for 3 days (or as per list below), but rinse at least twice every day.

During hotter weather, rinse more often. Thorough rinsing is important as the water provides the moisture needed to activate growth, it also flushes away waste products and re-oxygenates the seed, but be gentle.

To rinse, fill jar almost to the top with fresh cold water, swish around a little and drain well. Repeat, then return jar to cupboard. Note that sprouts like to stay moist, not too wet or too dry. After approximately 3 days the sprouts should be longer than the seed, which means they are ready to eat. Any seed or sprouts that are even slightly mouldy need to be discarded.

When ready, rinse sprouts well, drain and either return to the same jar, but with some paper towel in the bottom to prevent them sitting in water, or transfer to another well drained container with a regular lid and store in the fridge. They are best eaten within 3–4 days.

Sprouting containers

You can buy special sprouting containers in health food stores, but I just use a large glass jar with a wide neck. A clean chux or muslin (cheesecloth) fixed firmly with a rubber band, or something similar, provides the lid. The covering needs to allow sufficient ventilation, or you can end up with mouldy sprouts.

Lentil sprouts

Lentils are my favourite legume to sprout and if you are new to sprouting I encourage you to try these first. They are easy to sprout, always work, only take three days before they are ready to eat, plus they have a sweet, mild, nutty flavour and lovely crunchy texture. And when sprouted, lentils yield around six times their initial measure!

- Note: do not use split lentils, only whole lentils will sprout.

How to sprout lentils

1. Place 1/4 cup brown, French green or black Beluga lentils in a small bowl, cover with water and set aside overnight.
2. The next day drain and rinse well.
3. Transfer drained lentils into a roomy jar, place a breathable cover over the top, secure tightly, and place in a dark cool cupboard for the next 3 days, but rinse lentils at least once daily.
4. To rinse lentils, if the lid is secure enough, fill jar with water to cover lentils well, swish around gently, then tip the jar upside down and allow the majority of the water to drain out through the lid.
5. Repeat every day for 3 consecutive days. In very hot weather, you may want to do this twice each day.
6. After 3–4 days, when sprouts are lovely and long, rinse and use straight away or transfer to an airtight container and store in fridge for 3–4 days.
7. Makes 2-3 cups of sprouts.
8. Can be used in 'Sprouted spring salad' on page 134.

- While the risk of foodborne illness is very low, due to the inability to eliminate risk of contamination, it is suggested that populations 'at risk' should not consume raw sprouts: this includes the very young, elderly, pregnant, and those with compromised immune systems.

Sprout troubleshooting

- Sprouts are easy to grow but if you are having problems it might be due to:
- Overcrowding: Too many seeds in your sprouting container means that some seeds suffocate. This can cause sliminess, and ungerminated seeds could become mouldy.
- Oversoaking: Soaking for too long can kill a seed; it simply drowns.
- Not enough rinsing: Sprouts need to be rinsed regularly to prevent them drying out.
- Wrong time of year: Sprouts started at very high or very low temperatures risk failure.

It's summer! It's salad time

Spring and summer provide us with an abundance of fruit and vegetables and in Australia, we are spoilt for choice. Most of the vegetables available during the hotter months are perfect to be served as salads, as they are best prepared simply and either served raw, or only lightly cooked.

But when I say salad I'm not talking about a bit of greenery to garnish your plate. I'm talking about hearty, enticing meals. A dish that is full of fresh, vibrant, colourful vegetables, combined with lots of different textures from grains, legumes and/or nuts and seeds, topped off with an amazingly tasty and tangy dressing that brings it all together. Salads that are a delight to eat. Salads where each mouthful is different and interesting. Salads that can be served as a hearty main or a substantial side dish. Salads that you can eat for months on end without ever becoming bored or tired of, as the combinations are endless, and each and every bite provides maximum nutrition.

So what is the secret to making a plant-based salad truly hearty and more satisfying? It's the simple addition of a carbohydrate or protein element like wholegrains, legumes, nuts or seeds.

Whether they are the bulk of the salad, or just a small inclusion, nutritious wholegrains like barley, brown rice or quinoa are not only a fabulous low GI carbohydrate addition, but they add lovely textures, flavours and can boost fibre content. These types of salads have the added bonus that they often taste better the next day, which is not normally a feature of your more traditional salads.

The more waxy* styles of potatoes, all of which happen to be low GI when cold, are another fabulous carb-rich component, as are roasted sweet potato or corn. Of course if you don't have any of these to hand, you can always serve your salad with some fresh crusty chewy sourdough bread, which should also be used to mop up any leftover dressing. Mmmmm, delicious!

Legumes are another wonderful salad ingredient that have the advantage of being both a carb and a protein source, which is why you will find salads that include them more sustaining. I prefer to cook my own legumes, but using tinned ones are a super-easy and quick alternative, especially during hot days when you don't feel like lighting your stove. One benefit to cooking your own chickpeas, beans and lentils, though, is that if you dress them while still warm, they'll absorb more of the delicious flavours from the dressing,

For a salad to be more of a meal it requires a certain adherence to the basic principal of low GI carbohydrate, plus protein, plus fresh, seasonal vegetables. Of course, these don't have to be all in the same salad. I love to combine a few different salads on my plate to make a fabulous ensemble of vibrant colours, different flavours and lots of textures, all the while managing to get this balance. If you use the menu planner in the back of this book, you will see that I suggest a combination of salads to be served for dinner, which, when combined together, include all of these components. And I hope that any remains will be packed up and the enjoyment can continue when you get to munch on the delicious leftovers for lunch or dinner the next day.

veggie-licious

Amazing salads don't require you to stick to a recipe closely. You can easily substitute what you have on hand or what looked better at the market that day. Swap asparagus for green beans, use baby spinach leaves instead of rocket, and most grains and legumes can easily stand in for each other. This is just another way to ensure your salad combos are almost endless.

Possibly the most important aspect of your salad is to dress it with the best quality, Australian produced, extra virgin olive oil (EVOO) that you can afford. Why? Well apart from helping your salads taste amazing, extra virgin olive oil contains powerful plant antioxidants, in particular polyphenols, which can help to protect against heart disease and cancer, reduce rheumatoid arthritis symptoms, are beneficial for gut health, and even play a role in slowing the ageing process. All that, plus some phytonutrients in vegetables, such as carotenoids and glucosinolates, are better absorbed in the presence of dietary fat such as EVOO. In Australia we have some of the strictest standards in the world with regards to what can be labelled as extra virgin, so you can be guaranteed you are getting what it says on the tin. Personally I don't hold back and love to douse my salads in my latest favourite locally produced EVOO!

And finally, when it comes to the end of your savoury salad meal, why not top it off with a gorgeous fresh fruit salad (or platter) including a selection of stone fruit, melon and berries. The best that this season has to offer – which, by the way, is an equally great way to start the day!

A note on extra virgin olive oil (EVOO)

Extra-virgin olive oil (EVOO) comes from the first pressing of the olives without the use of heat or chemical treatments. It contains phytonutrients that are otherwise lost in the refining process. These include polyphenols that reduce the risk of heart disease (in part by preventing oxidation of cholesterol), carotenoids which decrease skin cancer risk, alpha tocopherol or vitamin E, an antioxidant which helps to protect the skin from sun damage, oleocanthal, which helps to reduce inflammation, lignans, which reduce breast cancer risk, and squalene, which can inhibit tumours.

EVOO, a monounsaturated fat, also does not oxidise (go rancid) as quickly as other fats, especially polyunsaturated, vegetable oils. Anything other than 'extra virgin' is refined, lower in quality and not linked with the same health benefits.

Contrary to the old belief that you couldn't cook with EVOO, actually, you can. Studies on Australian EVOO have shown that it is one of the most stable oils during cooking, even at very high temperatures (although I don't encourage that you heat it to such high temperatures). The high antioxidant content of EVOO actually helps to protect the oil as it is heated.

*Waxy varieties of potatoes which work best in salads include Nicola, kipfler, bintje, patrone, pink eye, pink fir, purple congo, Charlotte and spunta.

For more information on potato varieties go to the *Potatoes South Australia* website www.potatoessa.com.au and *The Diggers Club* www.diggers.com.au

How to make a good salad GREAT!

1 **DRESSING**
The dressing needs to have the right balance of acid (lemon juice or your choice of vinegar) and extra virgin olive oil. The amount of dressing used is also important. You need enough so you can taste it in each bite, but not too much so that you end up with a drowned, drippy salad. Ewww!

2 **FRESH HERBS**
The use of fresh herbs, especially in spring and summer, provide light, fresh, clean, vibrant flavours to salads. My favourite summer herbs to use are coriander, mint, basil, parsley and chives.

3. **TEXTURE**
The best salads have a blend of crisp and soft, as too much crisp is a bit onerous and too soft can be soggy and not enjoyable. And a little crunch from nuts and/or seeds is always welcome.

4. **SIMPLICITY**
Lastly, don't make your salads too busy. Keep it simple, but embellish by following the above three guides.

Eating seasonally spring/summer

Eating what is in season and grown close to home will allow you to enjoy food at its peak and have every ingredient bursting with nutrients and flavour. It is also a great way to be more in sync with the environment in which you live and support your body as it adapts to the changes in season.

Fruit and vegetables are at their best when they are in season. They taste better, are plentiful and are also cheaper. Not only will you be supporting the local farmers who grow this food, but eating seasonally encourages you to explore different recipes using the varying produce available, and will provide a natural variety to what you eat throughout the year.

Seasonal changes alter your metabolism and influence your food intake. In winter, cooler weather encourages greater food consumption to maintain body temperature. Appetite naturally increases as the body asks for more food to help it stay warm. By contrast, in spring and summer you get warmth from the sun, therefore have less need to produce internal heat and your appetite naturally decreases.

The fruit and vegetables available during each season support and provide you with the nutrients your body needs at that particular time of year. When the temperature is cooler most people tend to prefer heavier and heartier meals. As the weather gets warmer we are drawn towards lighter meals that need minimal or no cooking. The produce available in spring and summer is best prepared simply, using lighter cooking methods to keep it as fresh and raw as possible. Lightly cooked and raw foods are typically more refreshing as they help hydrate (they have a higher water content) and cool the body.

Spring Spring is a time of expansion. It brings longer days and warmer temperatures. Many animals and plants wake up from their wintery rest and it's the beginning of crop production season.

Foods to include in spring: leafy greens and lettuce, asian greens, sprouts, herbs like parsley and basil and use citrus to flavour and lighten meals.
Cooking methods: quick styles like blanching, pan frying and grilling.

Summer As the weather in summer becomes hotter, some areas in Australia can become very dry. People spend more time doing outdoor activities and it is a great time to eat outside. It is important to drink more and use more hydrating and cooling foods to prevent dehydration.

Foods to include in summer: cucumber, snow peas, leafy greens, berries, stone fruit and melons. Garnish salads and other dishes with cooling herbs like fresh coriander and mint.
Cooking methods: faster styles like stir frying, sautéeing and cooking on the barbecue.

On the following pages are lists of the fruit and vegetables that are at their best in spring and summer. I encourage you to base your meals around these.

Spring season food guide

fruit

- apple, lady william
- avocado
- banana
- blueberries
- cantaloupe
- cherry
- cumquat
- grapefruit
- honeydew
- kiwi fruit
- lemon
- lime
- loquat
- lychee
- mandarin, ellendale, imperial, murcot
- mango
- mulberries
- orange, blood, seville, valencia
- papaya
- pepino
- pineapple
- rhubarb
- strawberries
- starfruit
- tangelo
- watermelon

vegetables

- artichoke, globe, jerusalem
- asian greens, bok choy, choy sum, gai laan, wombok
- asparagus
- avocado
- beans, broad, green
- beetroot
- broccoli
- Brussels sprouts
- sprouts
- cabbage
- capsicum
- carrot
- cauliflower
- celery
- cucumber
- fennel
- kale
- leek
- lettuce
- mushrooms
- onion
- onion, spring
- parsnip
- peas
- peas, snow
- peas, sugar snap
- potato
- radish
- shallot
- silverbeet
- spinach
- squash
- sweetcorn
- tomato
- watercress
- zucchini

herbs

- basil
- basil, thai
- chervil
- chilli
- chives
- coriander
- dill
- garlic
- ginger

Summer season food guide

fruit

- apple, gravenstein
- apricot
- banana
- blackberries
- blueberries
- boysenberries
- cantaloupe
- cherries
- currants
- fig
- grapefruit
- grapes
- honeydew
- lemon
- loganberries
- lychee
- mango
- mulberries
- nectarine
- orange, valencia
- passionfruit
- peach
- pear, Bartlett and William
- plum
- pineapple
- rambutan
- raspberries
- rhubarb
- strawberries
- tamarillo
- watermelon

vegetables

- asparagus
- avocado
- beans, butter and green
- beetroot
- cabbage
- capsicum
- carrot
- celery
- corn
- cucumber
- daikon
- eggplant
- leek
- lettuce
- okra
- onion
- onion, spring
- peas
- peas, snow
- peas, sugar snap
- potato
- radish
- shallot
- silverbeet
- squash
- tomato
- watercress
- zucchini
- zucchini flower

herbs

- lime, kaffir (leaves)
- lemongrass
- mint
- mint, apple
- mint, Vietnamese
- oregano
- parsley
- rosemary
- sage
- tarragon
- thyme

spring & summer recipes

Dips
- Heavenly hommus
- Beetroot dip
- Muhumarra
- White bean dip with garlic and herbs

Burgers
- Black bean and quinoa burgers
- Eggplant and adzuki bean burgers
- Chickpea and lentil burgers with avocado salsa
- Okonomiyaki (Japanese pancake)

Wraps and stacks
- Coconut chapati, bean and salad stacks
- Fresh spring rolls
- Summertime rice paper rolls with peanut dipping sauce
- Quinoa and brown rice California rolls

Bean salads
- Marinated bean salad
- Black-eyed peas with garlic and lemon
- Black bean salad with corn and avocado
- Creamy potato salad with butter beans and mint

Lentil and chickpea salads
- Beetroot, lentil, feta and walnut salad
- Watercress salad with roasted capsicum, lentils and haloumi
- Greek salad with avocado and chickpeas
- Green goddess slaw with chickpeas

Grain salads
- Barley salad with tomatoes, feta and basil
- Barley and corn salad with miso dressing
- Quinoa, lentil and broccoli salad
- Brown rice salad

Veggie salads
- Super simple kale salad with a few variations
- Carrot, beetroot and mint salad
- Julienned summer veggie salad
- Sprouted spring salad

Mains
- Raw tomato sauce with zoodles
- Stir fried veggies with honey, soy and basil tofu
- Vegetable koftas with tomato and tamarind sauce
- Tomatoey eggplant and lentils on sweetcorn polenta

Something sweet
- Mango mousse
- Banana ice cream
- Carrot and quinoa cupcakes with tofu cashew 'cream'
- Peanut butter chickpea energy balls

Dips

Dips make a great snack served with veggies or grainy crackers, but I also love to use them as a spread on toast, in sandwiches and wraps or as a topping on burgers. Many of the dips available to buy contain fillers (breadcrumbs, potato) and undesirable oils, so always check the ingredients list. It is well worth the effort, plus it is quick and easy, to make your own. Here are four of my favourites.

Serving notes: All of these dips are delicious served with a mixture of vegetable crudités and healthy crackers. As it is difficult to find a healthy cracker to buy, I have included a great recipe for seedy crackers in the glossary. This recipe comes from my website, they are easy to make and perfect with any dip (as well as cheese!).

Heavenly hommus

I love lots of variety in my intake, but I will never get tired of eating hommus. Besides, it always tastes slightly different each time I make it, according to how strong the garlic is and how much lemon juice or tahini I add. It is super-easy to make using tinned chickpeas, however if you can cook your own chickpeas it is even better as the texture will be creamier. I have included my favourite five variations so you will never tire of eating this dip either!

Makes approx 1½ cups • prep time 10 mins • cook time 0 mins • serve with veggies • V • GF

400 gram tin chickpeas, drained and rinsed

1–2 cloves garlic

2 tablespoons (45 grams) tahini

2–3 tablespoons freshly squeezed lemon juice

¼–½ teaspoon salt

2–4 tablespoons water

To serve

extra virgin olive oil

sweet paprika, cumin or fresh herbs (parsley, chives, basil, dill)

vegetable crudités and/or healthy crackers

1. Place chickpeas, garlic, tahini, 2 tablespoons of lemon juice and ¼ teaspoon of salt in the bowl of a food processor and process until smooth. You may need to stop and use a spatula to wipe the sides down a few times while doing this.
2. When smooth, add 2 tablespoons of water and process until well mixed in and smooth.
3. Taste and add more garlic, lemon juice or salt as needed.
4. If still quite thick, add more water for a softer texture. It will thicken as it stands.
5. Serve drizzled with olive oil and sprinkled with paprika, cumin or any other spice or fresh herbs of choice.

FIVE HEAVENLY HOMMUS VARIATIONS

1. **Basil-pesto hommus** Add ½ cup fresh basil leaves, roughly chopped. Purée with dip or keep chunky. Alternatively, stir ¼ cup pesto (recipe in glossary) through hommus.
2. **Semi-dried tomato and basil hommus** Add ½ cup chopped semi-dried tomatoes and ½ cup fresh basil leaves, roughly torn.
3. **Roasted capsicum hommus** Add 1–2 roasted capsicums (see glossary for how to roast capsicums) roughly chopped; puree capsicum or keep chunky. You may also like to add ¼ cup fresh basil leaves.
4. **Moroccan hommus** Add 2 teaspoons each of ground cumin and ground coriander, or 1 tablespoon of Moroccan seasoning (ras-el-hanout); garnish with fresh coriander.
5. **Spiced-up hommus** Add chilli, harissa (a garlic and chilli paste), za'atar, or any other of your favourite spice blends plus some fresh herbs of choice (coriander, parsley, dill etc) for an interesting spicy hommus blend. Endless possibilities here alone!

EACH 45G (2 TBSPN) SERVING PROVIDES
66 calories (276 kilojoules), 3g protein, 4g fat, 0.5g saturated fat, 4g carbohydrate and 2g fibre

Beetroot dip

This is a great fall-back dip for when you have guests on the way and realise you have nothing to serve when they arrive. I always have tinned beetroot in my pantry as it is a great addition to most salads. Yoghurt and horseradish are two other ingredients to have in your fridge at all times. This dip can also be made with fresh, roasted beetroot when it is in season. I have included that version below.

Makes approx 1½ cups • prep time 5 mins • cook time 0 mins • serve with veggies • GF

400 gram tin beetroot, drained

1 teaspoon horseradish, or more to taste

1 tablespoon natural or Greek yoghurt, or more to taste

To serve

extra virgin olive oil

fresh dill or parsley

vegetable crudités, healthy crackers

1. Place beetroot, horseradish and yoghurt in bowl of a food processor and blend until smooth.
2. You may need to stop and use a spatula to wipe the sides down a few times while doing this.
3. Transfer to a serving bowl, drizzle with a little oil and sprinkle with fresh herbs.
4. Serve with vegetable crudités or healthy crackers

VARIATION

1. Make this dip using 2 medium fresh, roasted beetroot.
2. To roast beetroot, heat oven to 180 degrees and line a baking tray with non-stick paper. Trim any stalk from the top of the beetroot, scrub well with a vegetable brush and cut into small cubes, approx 2 cm in diameter (keep the skin on). Toss with a little extra virgin olive oil, salt and pepper and spread evenly over baking tray. Cook for 30 minutes, until beetroot is soft.
3. Transfer the beetroot to the bowl of a food processor. Blend until smooth. Add horseradish and yoghurt to taste.

COOK'S TIPS

- Dip will keep for up to 5 days in the fridge.
- For a vegan version, replace yoghurt and horseradish with ½ cup toasted walnuts and 1–2 tablespoons of pomegranate molasses.
- As well as being an excellent source of fibre, folate and a good source of the minerals manganese, potassium, copper and magnesium, beetroot are rich in antioxidant compounds called betalains that have anti-inflammatory and possibly blood pressure lowering effects in the body.

EACH 47G (2 TBSPN) SERVING PROVIDES
22 calories (91 kilojoules), 0.8g protein, 0g fat, 0g saturated fat, 4g carbohydrate and 1g fibre

Muhumarra

This is one of my favourite dips as the flavours are amazing and it is so delicious. It also looks fabulous as it has the most beautiful vibrant red colour. Muhammara (or mouhamara) is a traditional red capsicum (pepper) spread or dip originating from Syria. It can be used as a topping for veggie burgers as well as baked or pan-fried tofu, chicken or fish. If serving it this way it looks great a bit chunkier, like a pesto. When serving it as a dip, I like to purée it until it is quite smooth.

Makes approx 3 1/2 cups • prep time 20 mins • cook time 0 mins • serve with veg • V • GF

4 large red capsicums, roasted (350 grams of roasted flesh, approx)

1/2 large red chilli, chopped, seeds removed or a pinch of chilli powder, optional

2 cups (250 grams) walnuts, toasted

2-3 cloves garlic

2 tablespoons pomegranate molasses (see tips)

2 teaspoons ground cumin

1/2 teaspoon salt

1/2 cup whole rolled oats

1/4 cup extra virgin olive oil

To serve

extra pomegranate molasses

mint, pomegranate seeds, feta or walnuts

1. Place roasted red capsicums, chilli if using, walnuts, garlic, pomegranate molasses, cumin, salt and oats in a food processor. Process until mostly smooth. You may need to stop and use a spatula to wipe the sides down a few times while doing this.
2. Add olive oil slowly, while motor is running, and continue to process until smooth.
3. Tip into a serving bowl and garnish with a drizzle of pomegranate molasses and mint, pomegranate seeds, feta cheese or extra walnuts.

COOK'S TIPS

- You can replace the roasted capsicums with a 450 gram jar of whole roasted peppers, drained.
- This dip keeps for up to 1 week in the fridge.
- You can find pomegranate molasses at Middle Eastern and fruit and vegetable shops, and also in most supermarkets now. It has an amazing tart flavour. If you cannot find it, substitute with 2 teaspoons of honey plus 1 tablespoon freshly squeezed lemon juice.
- For a gluten free option, replace oats with 1/2 cup gluten free breadcrumbs
- Red capsicums are one of the richest dietary sources of vitamin C, which, when eaten with plant-based foods that are a source of iron, can boost iron absorption.

EACH 52G (1/4 CUP) SERVING PROVIDES
184 calories (773 kilojoules), 3g protein, 17g fat, 1g saturated fat, 5g carbohydrate and 2g fibre

White bean dip with garlic and herbs

A super-easy yet delicious dip which can also be used as a spread on sandwiches or wraps. The addition of fresh herbs makes it extra special. If you can, cook your own beans as the dip will turn out lighter and creamier.

Makes approx 1½ cups • prep time 10 mins • cook time 0 mins • serve with veggies • V • GF

- 400 gram tin cannellini or butter beans, drained and rinsed
- 1–2 cloves garlic
- 2 tablespoons extra virgin olive oil
- 1 tablespoon lemon juice
- ½ teaspoon salt
- 2 tablespoons flat-leaf parsley, roughly chopped

To serve

- 1 tablespoon fresh dill, roughly chopped
- 1 tablespoon fresh mint, roughly chopped
- vegetable crudités or healthy crackers

1. Place beans, garlic, 1 tablespoon oil, lemon juice and salt in the bowl of a food processor. Purée until smooth, stopping as needed to wipe down the sides of the bowl with a spatula.
2. Transfer to a serving bowl and stir through 1 tablespoon of parsley.
3. Drizzle with remaining oil and sprinkle with the remaining parsley, dill and mint to serve.
4. Serve with vegetable crudités and/or healthy crackers.

VARIATIONS

1. **White bean aïoli**
To above recipe add 1 extra tablespoon of lemon juice and 4 extra cloves of garlic and serve as a spread on a bun with any burgers in this book or as a super-garlicky dip with blanched green beans. YUM!

2. **White bean and basil dip**
Replace parsley, dill and mint with ½ cup fresh basil leaves, roughly chopped. Purée the basil with the dip or keep chunky. Alternatively replace herbs with ¼ cup pesto.

COOK'S TIPS

- Replace the tinned cannellini or butter beans with 240 grams (1⅓ cups) of cooked cannellini or butter beans.
- Not only do the fresh herbs help to add lovely fresh, delicate flavours to this dip, but they are also a potent source of antioxidants. Antioxidants are substances that can protect the human body from damage caused by unstable molecules known as free radicals. This protection includes reducing age-related wrinkles right through to preventing chronic illnesses such as heart disease and cancer.

EACH 38G (2 TBSPN) SERVING PROVIDES
42 calories (178 kilojoules), 2g protein, 2g fat, 0g saturated fat, 3g carbohydrate and 1g fibre

Burgers

Burgers are a great and tasty way to eat legumes and vegetables, and in the warmer months you can cook them on the barbecue. Serve either on a wholegrain bun with salad, or alongside any of the lovely salads included in this book. There are so many different veggie burgers you can make; here are just four of my favourites ones that I like to make in spring and summer.

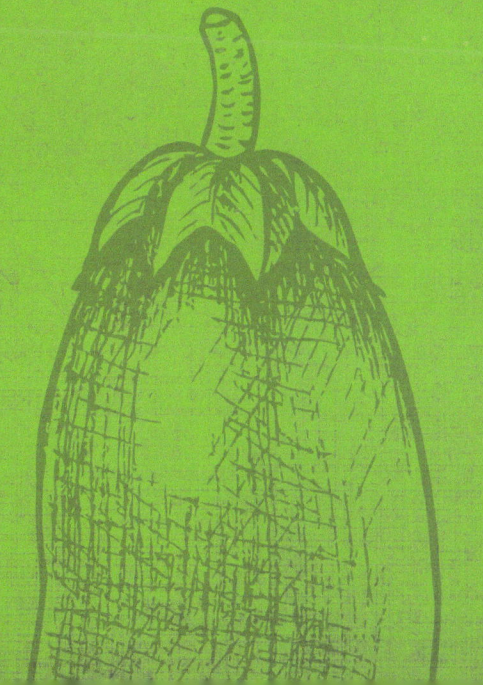

Black bean and quinoa burgers

These burgers are always a favourite when I make them in my cooking classes as they are so easy and very, very tasty. Trust me, even meat lovers will like them! Top with chilli jam, tomato relish or avocado salsa (see recipe included with chickpea burgers).

Makes 8 burgers • prep time 20 mins • cook time 15 mins • <1/2 serve of veg per burger • GF • V

- 3 tablespoons extra virgin olive oil
- 1 medium red onion, finely chopped
- 1 clove garlic, crushed
- 2 teaspoons ground cumin
- 400 gram tin black beans, drained and rinsed
- 1 cup cooked quinoa (refer to page 48 for how to cook quinoa)
- 1 medium zucchini, grated
- 4 tablespoons chickpea (besan) flour, plus extra as required
- 1/3 cup fresh coriander or parsley, chopped
- 3/4 teaspoon salt
- pepper, to taste

To serve

- chilli jam, tomato relish or avocado salsa
- wholegrain or gluten free rolls, optional
- salad of choice

1. Heat a frypan over medium heat. When hot add a drizzle of oil and the onion and sauté for 3–4 minutes, until the onion softens.
2. Add garlic and cumin and sauté for 1–2 minutes further.
3. Add black beans to the frypan and cook for 2 minutes.
4. Remove from heat and transfer black bean mixture into a large bowl and, using a fork or the back of a wooden spoon, lightly squash the beans. Mix in quinoa, zucchini, chickpea flour, parsley or coriander, salt and pepper. You may need to use your hands to do this!
5. Using a 1/4 cup measure, scoop out mix and flatten well to make the patties. Use a little extra chickpea flour to dust the outside and hold them together as necessary.
6. Heat the frypan over medium heat. When hot, add enough oil to cover the base of the pan, then add the burgers and cook for 3–4 minutes on each side, until golden brown. Note: do not skimp on oil while cooking the burgers as they can stick or burn very easily.
7. Transfer to a plate or tray covered with paper towel to remove any excess oil.
8. Serve topped with onion jam, tomato relish or avocado salsa on a bun (optional) and alongside one of the delicious salads in this book.

COOK'S TIPS

- Replace tinned black beans with 240 grams (approx 1 1/3 cups) cooked black beans, or any other bean (kidney, adzuki, cannellini, butter beans) or even chickpeas.
- Replace zucchini with carrot or pumpkin.
- Black beans with their deep dark colour are an excellent source of phytonutrients. Phyto (plant) nutrients are plant compounds with protective health benefits beyond those conferred by the vitamin and mineral content of plant foods. They slow the ageing process, reduce the risk of certain diseases and protect against some cancers.

EACH SERVING PROVIDES
154 calories (648 kilojoules), 5g protein, 8g fat, 1g saturated fat, 14g carbohydrate and 4g fibre

Eggplant and adzuki bean burgers

These are great tasting burgers with a fabulous soft texture thanks to the eggplant. Note that the mix is very soft when you first make it but will firm up as it stands. If you can, make the mix the day before and cook the burgers on the following day. Trust me, they are worth the effort!

Makes 16 burgers • prep time 90 mins • cook time 30 mins • 1/2 serve veg per burger • V • GF

½ cup adzuki beans

2–3 tablespoons extra virgin olive oil

1 medium brown onion, diced

2 medium eggplants, 600 grams approx, unpeeled cut into 2 cm pieces

¼ cup of water, or more as needed

2 cloves garlic, crushed

½ teaspoon ground cumin

½ teaspoon ground coriander

⅔ cup whole rolled oats

¼ cup fresh coriander or parsley, chopped

½–1 teaspoon salt

wholemeal or buckwheat flour, to coat

To serve

wholegrain bun, optional

salad

chutney or relish

1. Place adzuki beans in a medium saucepan and cover with plenty of water. Bring to the boil and cook, semi-covered, for approximately 30–40 minutes or until beans are soft.
2. Meanwhile, place a large frypan over medium heat. When hot, add a good tablespoon of oil along with the onion and eggplant and cook until softened, 10–15 minutes approx, adding water as necessary. If you have a lid you can use it to help the eggplant steam and speed up the cooking process.
3. When the eggplant is very soft and starting to brown slightly, add garlic, cumin and coriander and cook for a further 1–2 minutes.
4. Transfer mixture to the bowl of a food processor along with the beans, oats, fresh coriander and 1/2 tspn salt. Pulse until well combined, but not completely puréed as the mixture will become too sloppy. Taste and add extra salt as necessary.
5. Transfer to a bowl and refrigerate for at least 1 hour, or preferably overnight.
6. The next day, use a 1/4 cup measure to scoop out mix, mould into burgers and coat with flour.
7. Heat the frypan, add oil and cook burgers for 3–4 minutes either side until golden brown. When cooked, transfer to a plate or tray covered with paper towel.
8. Serve on a bun (optional) and alongside one of the delicious salads in this book.

COOK'S TIPS

- Replace the adzuki beans with the same quantity of black-eyed peas, which take a similar time to cook.
- Replace the dry adzuki beans with a 400 gram tin of cannellini or any other beans of choice. No need to cook, just drain and rinse.
- Add ½ cup of diced, roasted capsicum to the mix. Fold though just before putting the mix in the fridge.
- For a gluten free option, replace oats with ⅔ cup gluten free breadcrumbs or quinoa flakes and use buckwheat flour to coat.

EACH SERVING PROVIDES
73 calories (305 kilojoules), 2g protein, 3g fat, <0.5g saturated fat, 8g carbohydrate and 8g fibre

Chickpea and lentil burgers with avocado salsa

The recipe for these delicious burgers originally came from the Australian Egg Corporation website. I have changed it slightly. I like to serve them with an avocado salsa so have included the recipe, but they also team well with tzatziki or cucumber yoghurt, sweet chilli sauce or a tomato or mango relish.

Makes 14 burgers • prep time 20 mins • cook time 15 mins • 1/2 serve veg per burger

- 2–3 tablespoons extra virgin olive oil
- 1 large brown onion, diced
- 2 cloves garlic, crushed
- 2 teaspoons ground turmeric
- 2 teaspoons ground cumin
- 400 gram tin chickpeas, drained and rinsed
- 400 gram tin lentils, drained and rinsed
- ⅔ cup whole rolled oats
- ½ cup sunflower seeds
- ¼ bunch coriander
- 2 eggs, lightly beaten
- ½ teaspoon salt, optional
- pepper to taste
- wholemeal or buckwheat flour

Avocado salsa

- 1 medium ripe avocado, peeled and finely diced
- 1 large firm, tomato, finely diced
- ½ small Lebanese cucumber, finely diced
- ¼ red Spanish onion, peeled and finely diced or 2 spring onions, finely sliced
- 2 tablespoons fresh coriander, chopped
- 1 tablespoon lime or lemon juice
- salt and pepper to taste

EACH SERVING (BURGER ONLY) PROVIDES
116 calories (486 kilojoules), 5g protein, 7g fat, <1g saturated fat, 7g carbohydrate and 2g fibre

1. Place a frypan over medium heat. When hot, add a drizzle of oil and the onion and cook until softened, stirring occasionally.
2. Add garlic, turmeric and cumin and cook for a further 2–3 minutes while stirring.
3. Transfer mix to the bowl of a food processor. Add chickpeas, lentils, oats, sunflower seeds, coriander, eggs, salt and pepper and blend until smooth.
4. Using a 1/4 cup measure, scoop out mixture, mould into burgers and place on a plate dusted with flour.
5. Place a frypan over medium heat. When hot, add olive oil and chickpea burgers and cook for 2–3 minutes on each side, until golden brown. Transfer burgers to a plate covered with paper towel and keep warm while you repeat with remaining burgers.
6. Serve on or alongside a bun (optional) topped with avocado salsa and salad on the side.
7. For the avocado salsa, combine all ingredients in a bowl and stir gently. Store in the fridge until ready to serve.

COOK'S TIPS

- Chickpea burgers can be prepared ahead of time and stored in the fridge either uncooked or cooked for up to 5 days. Cooked burgers can be frozen.
- Salsa can be prepared ahead of time, but add the salt and pepper just before serving.
- For a vegan version, replace the 2 eggs with 2 portions of the linseed or chia egg replacer listed in the glossary.
- For a gluten free version, replace ⅔ cup oats with ⅔ cup gluten free crumbs and use buckwheat flour to dust on the outside.
- The addition of sunflower seeds and eggs to these delicious burgers helps to boost their protein content.

Okonomiyaki (Japanese pancake)

Okay, so not technically a burger, but these pancakes are so delicious I had to include them, and they are great in summer cooked on the flat grill of the barbecue. These are a great way to get kids to eat vegetables as they are jam-packed with them. Because they are so tasty, you will get demands for more. Plus, they can be served for breakfast, lunch or dinner!

Makes 8 pancakes • prep time 15 mins • cook time 20 mins • >1 serves of veg per pancake

¼ of a large (300 grams approx) cabbage, shredded (3 cups)

1 cup (110 grams) green beans, sliced into 3 cm lengths

½ medium red capsicum, sliced

1 medium zucchini (150 grams), halved lengthways and sliced thinly

1 medium carrot (130 grams), grated

½ cup fresh parsley, finely chopped

3 eggs

1 cup wholemeal flour

1 cup vegetable stock

pepper

firm tofu, optional

2 tablespoons extra virgin olive oil

To serve

sweet chilli sauce (mixed with a little water if quite thick)

1. Prepare the vegetables and parsley and set aside.
2. In a large bowl, whisk together eggs, then gradually add flour. Add the stock slowly and when fully mixed in and smooth, add the pepper.
3. Add vegetables and parsley into the batter and using a large spoon, mix well. If using tofu add now as well.
4. Heat a medium frypan (with a lid) over medium heat. When hot, add a good drizzle of oil and swish around to spread across base of pan.
5. Using a large spoon, spoon about ¾ cup of mixture into pan and flatten slightly with the back of the spoon. If you can fit more into the pan, do so, but leave some room in between so you can get a spatula under to flip them.
6. Place the lid on the pan and cook over medium–low heat until golden brown, about 3–4 minutes.
7. Carefully flip pancakes over and cook the other side for 3–4 more minutes.
8. Repeat with remaining batter.
9. Eat while still warm drizzled with a little sweet chilli sauce.

EACH SERVING PROVIDES
155 calories (649 kilojoules), 6g protein, 7g fat, 1g saturated fat, 14g carbohydrate and 5g fibre

COOK'S TIPS
96% of Australians don't eat the daily recommended amount of vegetables for good health. These pancakes will make it easy for you to eat yours!

Wraps & stacks

Bored with sandwiches for lunch? I have included four of my favourite, delicious alternatives, which can also be served as a light meal at dinner time.

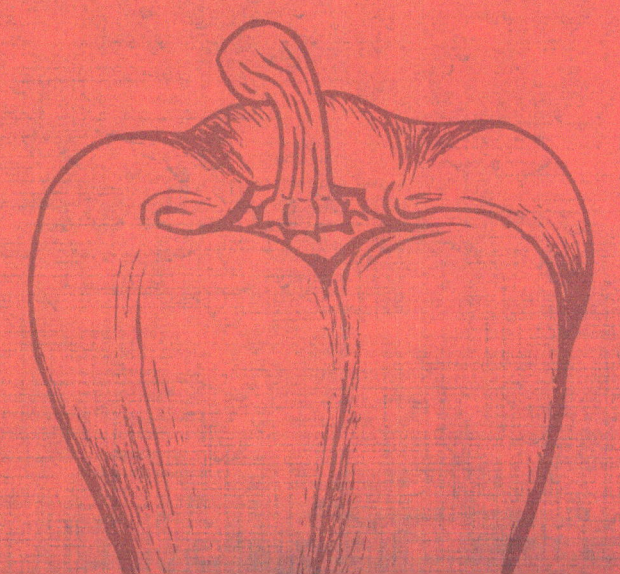

Coconut chapati and bean salad stacks

Too many years ago to admit to, when I was studying for my first science degree, I worked as a cook in a café where we made something similar to these. It is so long ago I couldn't remember the actual recipe, plus I felt it needed a bit of an update, but it went something like this ...

Serves 4 • prep time 20 mins • cook time 20 mins • 4 serves veggies per serve • V

For the chapatis

1 cup wholemeal flour
½ cup desiccated coconut
1 teaspoon baking powder
pinch of salt
½ cup warm water

For the toppings

400 gram tin of refried beans
⅔ cup tomato salsa (like Old El Paso) or sweet chilli sauce
100 grams baby spinach leaves or rocket
2 small carrots, skin on and grated
1 fresh beetroot, skin on and grated
2 tomatoes, sliced
1 medium ripe avocado, sliced
½ cup fresh coriander, roughly chopped

1. Combine flour, coconut, baking powder and salt in a medium-sized bowl.
2. Pour in water and mix to a smooth dough. Divide into 4.
3. Roll each quarter between two sheets of greaseproof paper to a 16 cm wide round disc.
4. Heat a frypan over medium heat. When hot add a chapati and cook for 3 minutes on each side until lightly browned.
5. Remove and repeat with remaining chapatis.
6. While chapatis are cooking, prepare the toppings.
7. Heat the refried beans, either carefully in a saucepan on the stove but make sure they don't stick, or in the microwave according to the directions on the tin.
8. To assemble chapatis, top each one with a quarter of the refried beans, then some salsa, salad, avocado and coriander. Enjoy!

COOK'S TIPS

- Want another great topping idea for these chapatis? Replace the refried beans and salsa with the kidney bean wrap filling on page 192. Mmmm, delicious!
- Refried beans are basically just mashed beans with some spices. You can make them yourself or buy them in tins already prepared. Check the ingredients list when buying your refried beans and look for brands that do not add oil, fat or lard. Refried beans are a great staple to have on hand in your pantry so that you can make these and many, many other quick and easy healthy meals.

EACH SERVING PROVIDES
373 calories (1566 kilojoules), 12g protein, 17g fat, 8g saturated fat, 38g carbohydrate and 13g fibre

Fresh spring rolls

These fresh spring rolls are similar to a very popular finger food we used to make at my café. I like the idea of making smaller-sized spring rolls because you get to eat more!

Makes 12 rolls • prep time 30 mins • cook time 15 mins • 1/2 serve of veg per serve

For the crêpes
2 large eggs
1 cup milk
½ cup wholemeal flour
pinch of salt

For the filling
1 tablespoon extra virgin olive oil
2 cloves garlic, crushed
150 grams firm tofu, sliced
1 medium carrot, julienned
1 medium zucchini, julienned
1 small red capsicum, julienned
80 grams snow peas, julienned
½ teaspoon sesame oil
½ cup fresh coriander
½ cup fresh mint
⅓ cup sweet chilli sauce
   plus 2 tablespoons water, if thick

1. Start by making the crêpe mixture: In a medium bowl whisk the eggs, add milk, then slowly mix in the flour, a little at a time to a smooth batter. Add salt and set aside for at least 10 minutes while you prepare the filling.
2. To make the filling: Heat a wok over medium heat. When hot add a drizzle of olive oil, 1 clove of garlic and tofu and cook for a few minutes until the tofu browns slightly. Remove and transfer to a large bowl.
3. Replace wok on heat, add another drizzle of oil, the second clove of garlic and the sliced vegetables.
4. Stir fry for a few minutes until slightly softened. Add sesame oil, stir through, then turn heat off and transfer veggies to the bowl with the tofu. Stir through coriander, mint and a drizzle of sweet chilli sauce (reserve the rest for dipping).
5. To cook crêpes: Heat a frypan over medium heat. When hot, add a drizzle of oil, using a brush or paper towel, wipe it around the pan, then add about 1/8 cup of the batter mixture and swirl around to cover the bottom of the pan. Cook until brown, then flip over and cook the other side for 1–2 minutes. Set aside and keep warm while cooking the remainder of the mixture.
6. To assemble spring rolls, fill each crêpe with some warm tofu and vegetable mixture and roll up.
7. Serve with sweet chilli dipping sauce.

EACH SERVING (PER FILLED CRÊPE) PROVIDES
99 calories (416 kilojoules), 5g protein, 5g fat, 1g saturated fat, 7g carbohydrate and 2g fibre

COOK'S TIPS
- Crêpes can be made up to 3 days ahead and stored in the fridge.
- These are a much healthier alternative to the usual deep-fried spring rolls, yet still incredibly tasty!

Summertime rice paper rolls with peanut dipping sauce

These rolls are the perfect summertime food. Light, crunchy, tasty and requiring minimal, if any, cooking. Not only is it fun making your own rolls, but you are forced to slow your pace of eating, allowing time to recognise when you are full (which can stop you from overeating). Plus the fillings can be varied as much as your imagination can manage, so they can be different every time you make them! The trick with helping your rice paper to stay in one piece – which I learned while in Vietnam - is to not leave the rice paper in the water for too long. Just wet it quickly, 3 or 4 seconds, it should still be quite firm when you remove it from the water and place it on your plate. It will soften in the time it takes to select your fillings and, when you are ready to roll, it will be the perfect consistency to roll without the paper splitting. Try it and you will see!

Makes 12 rolls • prep time 20 mins • cook time 0 mins • 1/2 serve of veg per roll • GF • V

For the peanut sauce

- 3 tablespoons crunchy peanut butter
- 1 tablespoon tamari or light soy sauce
- 2 teaspoons maple syrup or honey
- ¼ cup coconut milk
- 1–2 tablespoons water
- 2 tablespoons fresh coriander, roughly chopped

For the rolls

- 25 grams bean thread vermicelli noodles
- 1 medium avocado, sliced
- 2 medium carrots, julienned
- 1 red capsicum, julienned
- 1 Lebanese cucumber, julienned
- 1 cup fresh basil leaves
- 1 cup coriander leaves
- ⅓ cup toasted peanuts, roughly chopped
- 12 rice paper sheets

EACH SERVING (1 ROLL WITH SAUCE) PROVIDES
143 calories (600 kilojoules), 3g protein, 8g fat, 2g saturated fat, 14g carbohydrate and 2g fibre

1. To make the peanut sauce: Mix peanut butter, tamari, honey, coconut milk, water and coriander together and set aside.
2. To make the wraps: Boil the kettle. Place vermicelli noodles in a medium bowl, pour boiling water over to cover. Sit for 5 minutes, then drain.
3. Arrange all the fillings in the middle of the table for everyone to help themselves.
4. Half-fill a large bowl with warm water. Dip one wrapper in the water for a few seconds, and place on a plate.
5. Place some herbs and other fillings on the wrapper, about 3 cm from the base.
6. Sprinkle with peanuts, then fold up the bottom of the wrapper.
7. Fold in the sides and roll up firmly to enclose filling. Serve rice paper rolls with the dipping sauce.

COOK'S TIPS

- These are a lovely light lunch or dinner. For a more filling option, add pan-fried tofu to the filling.
- Bean thread or mung bean vermicelli noodles are a lower GI noodle. They are a type of transparent noodle made from mung bean, green bean starch, yam, potato starch, cassava or canna starch and water.

Quinoa and brown rice California rolls

The idea of using quinoa along with rice in these California rolls came from one of my lovely clients. Quinoa contains almost double the fibre of brown rice, helping to boost the fibre content of these rolls. It also helps to 'lighten' the rice a little.

Makes 12 rolls • prep time 20 mins • cook time 40 mins • 1/2 serve of veg per roll

1 cup long grain brown rice
2/3 cup white, red or tri-coloured quinoa
4 tablespoons rice vinegar
2 teaspoons sugar
6 nori sheets
2 teaspoons wasabi, optional
1/2 cup toasted sesame seeds
1 small Lebanese cucumber, sliced
1 medium avocado, sliced
2 carrots, grated
1 medium beetroot (120 grams), grated

To serve
tamari or light soy sauce for dipping

1. Start by cooking the brown rice and quinoa. Place the brown rice in a saucepan with 4 cups water, place lid on saucepan and bring to the boil. Lower the heat to a simmer and cook for 30–40 minutes.
2. To cook quinoa, place in a sieve and rinse well. Transfer into a saucepan with 2 cups water, place lid on saucepan and bring to the boil. Lower the heat to a simmer and cook for 12–15 minutes. When cooked, drain well, then fluff with a fork.
3. When cooked, mix together warm rice, warm quinoa, rice vinegar and sugar. Set aside to cool.
4. While you are waiting for the rice mixture to cool, prepare the fillings.
5. Place a sushi bamboo mat down on your bench with the slats running horizontally. Have a small bowl of water close by. Place nori sheet on sushi mat with the shiny side down and using the back of a teaspoon, spread a small amount of wasabi along the front edge of the nori sheet.
6. Measure out approx 1 cup of the quinoa and rice mix and, using wet hands, spread it evenly over the front 3/4 of the nori sheet, leaving at least a 3 cm-wide border along the edge furthest from you.
7. First sprinkle with 1 tablespoon of sesame seeds, then place cucumber along the front edge on top of the quinoa and rice, then follow with avocado, carrot and beetroot.
8. Roll nori sheet up.
9. When it is half rolled up, dip one of your hands in water and wet the end of the nori sheet. Continue rolling until all the filling is covered with the nori and you should have a neat roll. Repeat.
10. Cut the rolls in half or into bite sized pieces. Serve with soy dipping sauce. YUM!!!

EACH ROLL PROVIDES
184 calories (722 kilojoules), 5g protein, 7g fat, 1g saturated fat, 22g carbohydrate and 5g fibre

Bean salads

Bean salads are so easy to make — open a tin, toss together with a bunch of other tasty ingredients, add some fresh herbs, a tangy dressing and voila, done! Plus they are so versatile and travel well — a quick-to-make, flavoursome and filling dish to take to barbecues, on picnics, pack into lunch boxes, or simply serve as part of dinner for some added protein or as your low-GI carb.

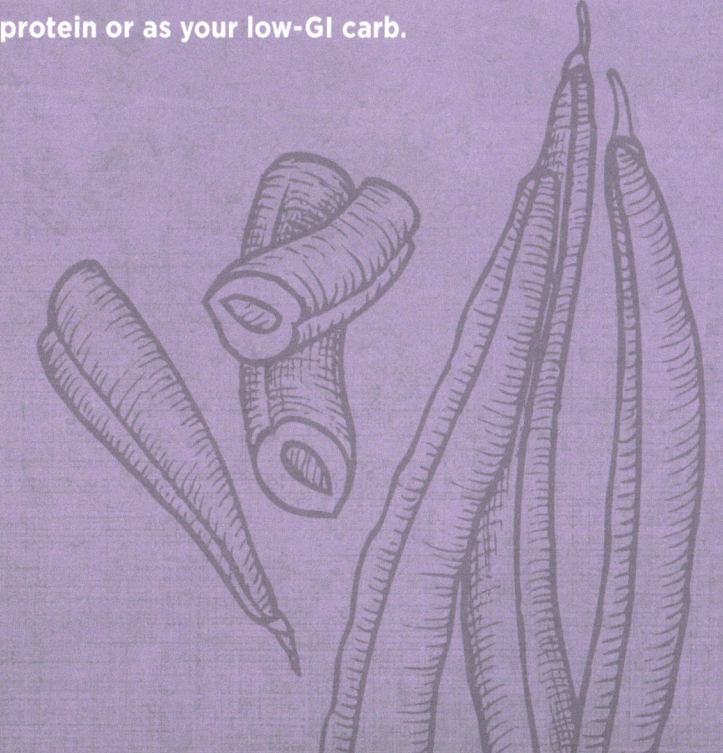

Marinated bean salad

This salad is an all-time favourite, partly because it gets tastier as it sits and the beans marinate in the delicious dressing, and partly because it is so adaptable. It is a great salad to take to a barbecue. It is also a great salad to take to work as you can make it on the weekend, and as it lasts for several days in the fridge, just remove a portion for lunch each day. If you can, add the spinach leaves and green beans just before serving to prevent them from wilting and discolouring.

Serves 4 as a side dish • prep time 10 mins • cook time 3 mins • 3 serves veg per serve • V • GF

- 420 gram tin of a 4- or 5-bean mix
- 2 tablespoons extra virgin olive oil
- 2 tablespoons apple cider vinegar or fresh lemon juice
- 2 cloves garlic, crushed
- ½ cup fresh basil leaves, torn or roughly chopped, plus extra for garnish
- ¼ cup green or black olives, pitted, or more as preferred
- 250 gram punnet smaller-sized cherry or grape tomatoes, cut in half if large
- 300g green beans, tops removed
- a few handfuls of baby spinach leaves (75 grams), optional

1. Drain and rinse the tin of 4-or 5-bean mix. Set aside.
2. Put olive oil, vinegar or lemon juice and garlic in a large bowl. Whisk together. Add bean mix, basil leaves, olives and tomatoes. Stir and set aside.
3. Place a saucepan of water over high heat and bring to the boil. When water is boiling, add the green beans and cook for 3 minutes (or cook in a steamer basket). Rinse under cold running water to stop the cooking process, then add to the salad and toss through.
4. Place baby spinach leaves in the bottom of a serving bowl and tip bean salad on top. Garnish with extra basil leaves.

VARIATIONS

Any of the following can also be added to the salad:

- 1/2 cup roasted red capsicum, chopped
- 1 jar (280 grams, approx 9) artichoke hearts (in brine), drain and cut in half
- 1 bunch asparagus. Break woody stems off the bottom, cook the asparagus in the steamer for 3 minutes. Refresh under cold water when cooked
- 1/2 cup semi-dried tomatoes
- 1/2–1 cup roasted eggplant or zucchini
- 1/2–1 cup roasted pumpkin
- 1/4 –1/2 cup feta cheese to sprinkle on top

EACH SERVING PROVIDES
184 calories (772 kilojoules), 7g protein, 10g fat, 1g saturated fat, 13g carbohydrate and 8g fibre

COOK'S TIPS

Replace bean mix with a tin (or 1⅓ cups cooked) of cannellini beans, lentils or chickpeas, or any combination of these.

Black-eyed peas with garlic and lemon

This lovely, simple, light salad is based on a traditional Greek recipe and can be adapted in so many different ways. Black-eyed peas are an easy bean (pea) to cook yourself as they do not need to be pre-soaked, and cook in only 30–40 minutes. Plus they look great! This recipe will keep in the fridge for 3–4 days.

Serves 4 as a side dish • prep time 10 mins • cook time 40 mins • 1½ serves veg per serve • V • GF

- 1 cup (200 grams) dried black-eyed peas
- 1 small red onion, sliced thinly or 3 spring onions finely sliced
- ¼ cup freshly squeezed lemon juice
- 1 clove garlic, peeled and crushed
- ½ teaspoon salt
- freshly ground black pepper
- ⅓ cup extra virgin olive oil
- ½ cup fresh chopped parsley

1. Place black-eyed peas in a large saucepan with a lid and cover with plenty of water. Bring to the boil, then turn heat down and cook, semi-covered, for approximately 30–40 minutes or until beans are tender. You need to keep the peas under water at all times, so top with boiling water from the kettle as needed.
2. Meanwhile, place onion/s in a large bowl and add lemon juice, garlic, salt and pepper and stir to combine. This will allow the onion/s to soften and become milder in flavour
3. When cooked, drain and rinse the peas. Add to bowl with onion, then add olive oil and parsley and stir to combine. I like to serve this salad warm.

VARIATIONS

Any of the following can also be added to the salad:
- Blanched green beans
- Olives, sundried tomatoes and baby spinach leaves
- Feta cheese, olives and diced cucumber
- Feta cheese, olives and diced red capsicum
- Avocado and blanched asparagus

COOK'S TIPS

- Black-eyed peas are also available in tins. You will need two tins to replace the dried beans.
- You can cook the dry black-eyed peas in a pressure cooker. Rinse unsoaked peas. Add to a pressure cooker and cover well with water. Secure lid and bring up to pressure. Cook for 5 minutes. Remove from heat and allow the pressure to come down naturally. Or cook for 7 minutes with fast release.
- Black-eyed peas and other smaller beans are often better tolerated by those who suffer from a lot of gas when eating beans.

EACH SERVING PROVIDES
212 calories (891 kilojoules), 8g protein, 13g fat, 2g saturated fat, 14g carbohydrate and 7g fibre

Black bean salad with corn and avocado

For some reason this salad reminds me of Mexico, even though I have never been there! Not only is it visually striking due to the bright red, yellow and green on a black background, but it has the most beautiful flavour thanks to the fresh herbs.

Serves 6 as a side • prep time 10 mins • cook time 3 mins • 2½ serves veg per serve • V • GF

- 2 x 400 gram tins black beans, drained and rinsed
- 1 small red onion, finely diced or 2 spring onions, sliced
- 1 small red capsicum, diced
- 1 bunch fresh coriander, leaves and stems finely chopped (reserve some leaves for garnish)
- ½ bunch fresh mint, leaves picked and finely chopped
- 1 cob corn, husks still attached
- 1 punnet cherry tomatoes, halved
- 1 large ripe avocado, halved, flesh diced and scooped out gently

Dressing

- ¼ cup extra virgin olive oil
- ¼ cup lime or lemon juice (approx 2 limes or 1 larger lemon)
- 1 clove garlic, crushed
- ½ tsp salt
- freshly ground black pepper

1. Combine the black beans, onion, capsicum, coriander and mint in a large mixing bowl.
2. Add ingredients for dressing to a jar with a tight fitting lid and shake well to combine.
3. Pour dressing over the black beans and stir through to evenly coat. Taste to check seasoning.
4. Cook the corn with the husks still attached in the microwave on high for 3 minutes. Set aside to cool.
5. When cool enough to handle, remove husks from corn cobs, then carefully slice kernels off the cob and add to the salad.
6. Just before serving, gently stir the tomatoes and avocado through the salad.
7. Transfer salad to a serving platter or bowl and serve garnished with remaining coriander leaves.

VARIATION

Black bean and mango salad Replace the tomatoes, corn and avocado with 1 large ripe mango, which has been diced.

COOK'S TIPS

- Replace tinned black beans with 480 grams (2⅔ cups approx) cooked black beans.
- Add a small cucumber, diced.
- Replace fresh red capsicum with roasted capsicum.
- Add baby spinach leaves and/or rocket leaves to the salad.
- If your avocado is very ripe, instead of stirring it through the salad, serve with slices of avocado on top.
- If time poor, use 1 cup frozen corn kernels. Blanch for 2–3 minutes in boiling water first. Or use 1 cup tinned corn kernels, drained and rinsed.
- All the different colours in plant foods refer to different types of phytonutrients (a type of antioxidant). All phytonutrients have different disease-protecting effects in the body and they work together as a team to protect your health. This salad makes it easy to include lots of bright colours on your plate including reds, yellow and greens along with, of course, black!

EACH SERVING PROVIDES
185 calories (779 kilojoules), 6g protein, 16g fat, 3g saturated fat, 16g carbohydrate and 6g fibre

Creamy potato salad with butter beans and mint

This potato salad is a healthier version of my nanna's delicious potato salad. It is a favourite of mine from childhood. My nanna, Elsie, always added butter beans to her potato salad along with loads of fresh mint, chives and parsley from her garden. I have replaced her traditional mayonnaise dressing with a healthier version using yoghurt as a base.

Serves 6 as a side • prep time 45 mins • cook time 25 mins • 3 serves veg per serve • GF

- 1 kilogram medium sized Nicola, kipfler or other waxy potatoes, skin on, scrubbed well
- 400 gram tin butter (lima) beans
- 1 small red onion, finely diced or 4 spring onions, finely sliced
- ¾ cup natural or Greek yoghurt
- 1 tablespoon extra virgin olive oil
- 1 tablespoon lemon juice or apple cider vinegar
- 2 teaspoons Dijon mustard
- ½ cup fresh parsley, finely chopped
- ½ cup fresh mint, finely chopped, plus a few whole leaves extra for garnish
- 1 bunch chives, finely chopped, reserve 1 tablespoon for garnish
- 1 teaspoon salt
- pepper, to taste

1. Place whole potatoes in a large pot and cover with cold water Place over high heat and bring to the boil. Turn down to a simmer and cook until potatoes are tender, 15–20 minutes approx, depending on the size of your potatoes. Note: keep a close eye on them so they do not overcook and become mushy.
2. Drain and set aside to cool (this can be done the day before). When cool, slice into evenly-sized chunks.
3. While the potatoes are cooking and cooling, drain the tinned beans, rinse well and set aside.
4. For the dressing, into a large bowl, add the onion, yoghurt, oil, lemon juice or vinegar, mustard, parsley, mint, chives, salt and pepper and whisk together well.
5. When they have cooled, add the potatoes along with the beans to the yoghurt dressing and stir gently to combine.
6. Garnish with extra mint and chives. This salad keeps well for up to 4 days.

COOK'S TIPS

- You can replace the tinned beans with 240 grams (or 1⅓ cups) of cooked lima beans or cannellini beans.
- When cooking potatoes for salad, always start the potatoes in cold water that you bring to the boil. If you start them in boiling water, they will cook unevenly. The outside of the potato can become overcooked and mushy, while the inside stays undercooked; not at all what you want for your salad!
- Nicola potatoes are naturally a low GI potato, but all potatoes are low GI when served cold.

EACH SERVING PROVIDES
200 calories (840 kilojoules), 8g protein, 4g fat, <1g saturated fat, 29g carbohydrate and 6g fibre

Lentil & chickpea salads

Lentils are one of my favourite legumes to work with as you don't need to soak them and they only take 15–20 minutes to cook. If you are time poor, tinned brown lentils are a great option. However, do try cooking the French green and black Beluga ones at least once if you can. Chickpeas are a great addition to almost any salad. Their smooth, buttery texture teams well with fresh crunchy vegetables, plus they look fabulous!

Beetroot, lentil, feta and walnut salad

This is a really quick salad which is made mostly from ingredients which you should always have on hand in your pantry – olive oil, balsamic vinegar, tinned lentils and tinned beetroot. It is a fantastic salad to serve at a summer barbecue, or a tasty lunch to take to work.

Serves 4 as a side • prep time 10 mins • cook time 0 mins • 2 serves veg per serve • GF

- 1 tablespoon extra virgin olive oil
- 1 tablespoon balsamic vinegar
- 400 gram tin lentils, drained and rinsed
- 150 grams rocket and/or baby spinach leaves
- 425 gram tin baby beetroot, drained
- 100 grams feta cheese, crumbled
- ⅓ cup walnuts, either raw or toasted and broken
- ¼ cup fresh mint leaves, torn, optional
- pepper to taste

1. In a small bowl, whisk together olive oil and balsamic vinegar, then add the drained lentils and mix to coat. Set aside.
2. On a large platter, arrange the rocket and/or spinach leaves and drained beetroot.
3. Spoon the lentils evenly over the salad and drizzle with any extra dressing.
4. Crumble the feta over, sprinkle with the walnuts and garnish with mint leaves. Add pepper to taste. Serve and enjoy!

COOK'S TIPS

- Replace tinned beetroot with fresh cooked baby beetroot, available in most fruit and vegetable grocers and supermarkets; or replace tinned beetroot with 3 fresh beetroots, diced or cut into wedges and roasted with olive oil, salt and pepper until soft.
- Replace tinned lentils with 1⅓ cups home cooked brown, French green or black Beluga lentils.
- Add blanched green beans to the salad.
- For a vegan option, either omit feta cheese and add extra walnuts, or replace feta with a vegan cheese.
- Walnuts not only provide a lovely crunch to this salad, but are also an excellent source of the essential omega 3 fat, alpha-linolenic acid (ALA), called essential because it is necessary for health. It cannot be produced within the human body so it must be acquired through what we eat.

EACH SERVING PROVIDES
245 calories (1028 kilojoules), 13g protein, 16g fat, 3g saturated fat, 11g carbohydrate and 5g fibre

Watercress salad with roasted capsicum, lentils and haloumi

This salad was inspired by a visit to a most delicious Syrian restaurant called Almond Bar in Darlinghurst, Sydney, but I have adapted it slightly. It is very easy to make, especially if you use pre-roasted capsicums and tinned lentils. Lentils are an excellent source of fibre, plus they are a low GI carbohydrate food (so will keep you full for a long time) and a low-fat source of protein. Capsicums are beautifully sweet when roasted. Many people who cannot tolerate raw capsicum don't seem to have a problem when it is roasted.

Serves 4 • prep time 15 mins • cook time 5 mins • 1½ serves veg per serve • GF

2 red capsicums, roasted (see glossary)
4–6 cups or approx 100 grams watercress sprigs, washed well and dried
⅓ cup fresh mint leaves
100 grams haloumi
400 tin brown lentils, drained

Dressing
¼ cup extra virgin olive oil
¼ cup freshly squeezed lemon juice
1 clove garlic, crushed
pepper, to taste

1. Cut the roasted capsicum flesh longways into 3 mm lengths.
2. Remove any thick stalks from the watercress and wash along with the mint leaves. Use a salad spinner to dry, then set aside. Slice haloumi and set aside.
3. To make the dressing, place oil, lemon juice, garlic and pepper in a jar with a tight fitting lid and shake well to combine. As the haloumi is salty you should not need to add any salt.
4. Just before serving, place a frypan over medium heat. When hot, add the haloumi and cook for 2–3 minutes each side until browned.
5. Combine capsicum, lentils, watercress and mint in a serving bowl and pour the dressing over the top. Toss together and arrange on a serving platter. Top with haloumi and serve.

VARIATIONS
- For a faster version of this salad, use roasted red peppers, available in jars at delis and supermarkets
- Replace haloumi with buffalo mozzarella (no cooking needed)
- For a vegan option, replace cheese with a vegan cheese or walnuts

COOK'S TIPS
- Do ahead: Cook lentils the day before. Make dressing and pour over. Store in the fridge. You can roast the capsicums and store in fridge for up to 1 week or they can be frozen for up to 3 months.
- Watercress is rich in antioxidants that protect skin against ageing, eyes from macular degeneration and your whole body from cancer. Watercress belongs to the cruciferous family of vegetables along with broccoli, cauliflower, kale, Brussels sprouts, Chinese cabbage and rocket, well-known for their nutrient density and anti-cancer properties. In fact, watercress is reported to be even more nutrient dense than (the currently very popular) kale!

EACH SERVING PROVIDES
246 calories (1035 kilojoules), 10g protein, 19g fat, 5g saturated fat, 8g carbohydrate and 4g fibre

Greek salad with avocado and chickpeas

I love Greek salad and think it is a great side dish that teams well with almost anything. By adding avocado and chickpeas, this salad becomes a complete meal which can be eaten on its own. Oh, okay, with some lovely crusty sourdough bread to mop up the juices!

Serves 4 as a side • prep time 15 mins • cook time 0 mins • 3 serves veg per serve • GF

400 gram tin chickpeas, drained and rinsed

2 tablespoons extra virgin olive oil

2 tablespoons lemon juice

1 small clove garlic, crushed, optional

3 roma tomatoes, chopped, or 1 punnet cherry or grape tomatoes, halved if large

1 small Lebanese cucumber, diced

½ small red onion, finely sliced

12 pitted black or Kalamata olives

3–4 cups your choice of salad leaves, roughly chopped if large

1 medium avocado, sliced

80 grams feta cheese, diced

½ cup fresh dill, parsley or chives, chopped

1. Place chickpeas in a large bowl.
2. Add the extra virgin olive oil, lemon juice and garlic and mix to coat.
3. Add tomatoes, cucumber, red onion and olives to the bowl and stir through to combine.
4. Place salad leaves in the base of a serving bowl, top with chickpea salad, avocado and feta cheese.
5. Sprinkle with fresh dill or other herbs of choice.

COOK'S TIPS

- For a vegan option, replace feta with vegan cheese, or nuts, or omit altogether.
- Healthy monounsaturated fat in both avocado and extra virgin olive oil assists with absorption of certain phytonutrients in vegetables, such as carotenoids, which may help prevent skin, breast, and prostate cancer, as well as promote healthy vision and cell growth; and glucosinolates which reduce inflammation in the large bowel and may lower your risk of bladder, breast, bowel and other types of cancer.

EACH SERVING PROVIDES
293 calories (1232 kilojoules), 9g protein, 22g fat, 5g saturated fat, 13g carbohydrate and 6g fibre

Green goddess slaw with chickpeas

This is a gorgeous dressing that can be used on any other salad, drizzled over roasted vegetables or served my favourite way, with sweet potato 'fries' (that's baked 'fries' of course!)

Serves 6 • prep time 30 mins • cook time 0 mins • 3 veg per serve • GF

Green goddess dressing

- ½ avocado
- 1 clove garlic, crushed
- 2 teaspoons Dijon mustard
- 2 teaspoons honey
- ½ cup (120 grams) natural or Greek yoghurt
- 1½ tablespoons lemon juice
- 1 cup loosely packed basil leaves
- ½ cup loosely packed mint leaves, plus extra for garnish
- ⅓ cup loosely packed flat-leafed parsley
- ¼ cup water
- ¼ teaspoon salt
- pepper (to taste)

Coleslaw

- ¼–½ cabbage (400 grams approx), shredded
- 3 medium carrots (400 grams approx), grated
- 400 gram tin chickpeas, drained and rinsed
- 2–3 handfuls (100g) baby spinach leaves
- ¼ cup sunflower seeds

1. For the dressing: Add avocado, garlic, mustard, honey, yoghurt, lemon juice, basil, mint and parsley to the bowl of a food processor. Purée until smooth. You may need to stop and wipe the sides down. Add water to thin as necessary. Set aside.
2. To make the salad: Finely shred cabbage, grate carrots and combine in a large bowl along with chickpeas and half of the spinach leaves. Pour dressing over and toss to mix well.
3. Place remaining spinach leaves on the base of a serving platter, top with coleslaw, sprinkle with sunflower seeds and mint leaves and serve.

COOK'S TIPS

- To save on time you can use precut coleslaw (shredded cabbage and carrot) from the supermarket.
- Leftover Green goddess dressing keeps in the fridge for up to 1 week.
- Cabbage is a member of the cruciferous (or brassica) family of vegetables. It has anti-inflammatory effects in the body and can reduce your risk of bladder, breast, bowel, liver, lung and stomach cancer!

EACH SERVING PROVIDES
193 calories (809 kilojoules), 8g protein, 10g fat, 2g saturated fat, 15g carbohydrate and 9g fibre

Grain salads

I love the invigorating blend of textures and flavours wholegrains can add to salads. The following recipes showcase three of my favourite wholegrains I like to use in salads. The first two salads use pearl barley (okay, technically not a wholegrain, but very, very close) which has a lovely chewy texture and slightly nutty flavour. It is incredibly low GI and very filling. It is a superb, versatile and cheap but very underutilised grain. Hopefully you will start to use it from now on! I've also included a gorgeous quinoa salad and my favourite ever brown rice salad. Both grains make great bases for these more substantial and deliciously tasty salads. Enjoy.

Barley salad with tomatoes, feta and basil

Barley is one of my favourite grains to use, especially in salads. It tastes great, is cheap, has a lovely nutty flavour and chewy texture. It can be used to make risottos, soups and salads, like this one, which is one of my favourite quick and easy salads. This recipe originally came from taste.com.au but I have adapted it slightly. I love its simple yet amazing blend of textures and flavours.

Serves 6 • prep time 20 mins • cook time 40 mins • almost 1 serve of veg per serve

1 cup pearl barley

⅓ cup pine nuts

½ cup pitted Kalamata olives, halved

250 grams punnet cherry tomatoes, cut in half if large (or grape or pear tomatoes)

100 grams rocket or baby spinach leaves

80 grams feta, crumbled

Dressing

1 clove garlic, crushed

¼ cup lemon juice (juice of approx 1 lemon) or apple cider vinegar

¼ cup extra virgin olive oil

½ cup roughly chopped fresh basil, plus a few extra leaves for garnish

1. Place barley in a saucepan with 1.5 L (6 cups) water, cover with lid and bring to the boil. Turn down the heat and simmer for approximately 25–40 minutes or until just tender. Drain well.
2. Toast the pine nuts in a pan with a drizzle of oil for a few minutes until they become golden brown. Set aside.
3. To make the dressing, place garlic, lemon juice and oil in a screw-top jar and shake well.
4. Place the cooked barley in a large mixing bowl and pour over dressing, add basil and toss gently to combine.
5. Add olives, tomatoes, rocket and feta cheese. Sprinkle with pine nuts just before serving.

VARIATIONS

- Use pesto in place of fresh basil in the dressing
- Use bocconcini cheese in place of feta cheese
- Add avocado or roasted capsicum
- Use spelt berries or freekah in place of barley
- For a gluten free option, replace barley with a mixture of buckwheat and quinoa
- For a vegan version, replace feta with a vegan cheese or omit altogether and add extra pine nuts

COOK'S TIPS

- To cook barley in the pressure cooker, add 3 cups of water to 1 cup of barley and cook under pressure for 5 minutes.
- Given that olives and feta are quite salty, there is no need to add salt to this salad.
- Barley is full of soluble fibre, which can lower your cholesterol, and resistant starch, to lower your bowel cancer risk and feed the good bacteria in your gut.

EACH SERVING PROVIDES
322 calories (1354 kilojoules), 7g protein, 21g fat, 4g saturated fat, 24g carbohydrate and 6g fibre

Barley and corn salad with miso dressing

This salad, which is really popular in my cooking classes, was based on one I had in a café in Melbourne quite a few years ago. Sadly the café is no longer there. Their salad had a creamy miso dressing as they had blended the avocado with the dressing. I prefer to add it in fresh chunks as I love all the different textures this salad has.

Serves 6 • prep time 20 mins • cook tim 40 mins • 1½ serves of veg per serve • V

- 1 cup (200 grams) pearl barley
- 1 cob corn, with husk attached
- 1 tablespoon extra virgin olive oil
- 1 large or 2 small zucchinis, sliced, or when in season use 2 bunches asparagus, cut into 3 cm lengths
- 2–3 cups (100 grams) baby spinach leaves
- 1 ripe avocado, diced
- 1 bunch chives, finely chopped
- 2 tablespoons sesame seeds, toasted

Miso dressing

- 1½ tablespoons miso
- 2 tablespoons brown rice vinegar
- 1½ tablespoons tamari or light soy sauce
- 1 tablespoon extra virgin olive oil

1. Add the barley to a medium saucepan with plenty of fresh water to cover. Cook for 25–40 minutes or until soft but firm to the bite. Drain and set aside.
2. Meanwhile, cook the corn cob (with the outside husk still attached) in the microwave for 3 minutes. Allow to cool for 5 minutes before peeling off the husk, then carefully slicing off all of the corn kernels.
3. Heat a medium sized frypan that has a lid over medium heat. When hot, add a drizzle of olive oil, then add the corn and toss around to coat in the oil.
4. Add the zucchini or asparagus, place the lid on the pan (as the corn cooks, it will pop and 'jump out' of the pan) and cook until the corn browns, 4–5 minutes, tossing occasionally.
5. When corn has browned, remove vegetables from the pan into a bowl and set aside.
6. To make the dressing: Place miso in a jar with a tight fitting lid. Slowly add the vinegar and, using a spoon, mix into the miso to loosen the paste. Add the tamari and olive oil. Screw the lid on tight and shake well until all ingredients are well blended.
7. When the barley is cooked, pour dressing over the barley and mix well to coat. Stir corn and zucchini or asparagus through dressed barley. Then add spinach leaves and avocado. Mix gently until just combined. Transfer to a serving bowl and sprinkle with chives and sesame seeds just prior to serving. Enjoy.

COOK'S TIPS

- Miso is a Japanese paste made by mashing soy beans with a grain (my favourite one is rice), adding a culture and allowing the 'mash' to ferment for anywhere from 3 months to 3 years.
- Miso is a great source of probiotics, the type of good bacteria that we have in our gut.

EACH SERVING PROVIDES
287 calories (1207 kilojoules), 7g protein, 16g fat, 3g saturated fat, 26g carbohydrate and 7g fibre

Quinoa, lentil and broccoli salad

This salad, a delicious blend of quinoa, lentils and broccoli, along with crunchy seeds and nuts, is incredibly tasty. You first mix in loads of herbs and a lovely lemony dressing, then serve the salad topped with a cumin and honey yoghurt. You must give it a go as it looks stunning and is just delicious!

Serves 6 • prep time 20 mins • cook time 20 mins • 2 serves of veg per serve • GF

½ cup French green lentils

1 cup quinoa

2 heads of broccoli (500 grams approx), cut into florets

1 cup thick Greek yoghurt

1 teaspoon ground cumin

1 tablespoon honey

1 bunch coriander, leaves and stalks, finely chopped, reserve a little for garnish

½ bunch parsley, leaves and smaller stalks, finely chopped

3 spring onions, sliced

½ cup raisins

¼ cup lemon juice (approx 1 lemon)

¼ cup extra virgin olive oil

½ teaspoon salt

2 tablespoons pumpkin seeds, toasted

2 tablespoons sunflower seeds, toasted

2 tablespoons pine nuts, cashews, hazelnuts or other nuts, toasted

seeds from 1 pomegranate

2 handfuls (50 grams approx) baby spinach leaves

1. Rinse lentils, place in a saucepan and cover with boiling water. Cook for 20 minutes, or until firm but soft when you press one between your fingers.
2. Rinse quinoa then place in a saucepan with 3 cups of boiling water. Cover and cook for 12–15 minutes.
3. When cooked, drain both quinoa and lentils and set aside to cool.
4. Steam broccoli for 3–4 minutes, until cooked but still a little firm to the bite. Set aside.
5. Meanwhile, mix the yoghurt, cumin and honey together until well combined and set aside.
6. In a large bowl, add the coriander, parsley, spring onions, raisins, lemon juice, oil, salt, cooked quinoa, cooked lentils and broccoli. Mix well.
7. Just before serving, fold through the pumpkin seeds, sunflower seeds and toasted nuts.
8. Toss through baby spinach leaves and half the pomegranate seeds and place in serving dish. Top with yoghurt dressing, reserved coriander and remaining pomegranate seeds. Enjoy.

COOK'S TIPS

- While steaming broccoli is quick and easy, my favourite way to cook broccoli for this salad is to roast it.
- You can use other grains in place of quinoa including freekah (a green wheat), pearl barley, wheat or spelt berries.
- For a vegan version, replace yoghurt with a tahini and lemon dressing and the honey with maple syrup.
- Broccoli is a member of the brassica or cruciferous group of vegetables which are rich in many heath promoting nutrients. In particular, broccoli contains several carotenoids (beta-carotene, lutein, zeaxanthin); vitamins C, E, and K; folate; and minerals. It is also an excellent source of fibre.

EACH SERVING PROVIDES
313 calories (1879 kilojoules), 18g protein, 18g fat, 3g saturated fat, 49g carbohydrate and 12g fibre

Brown rice salad

This is the most delicious brown rice salad I have ever eaten. A friend kindly shared this recipe with me many years ago, but could never remember which of her cookbooks she got it from. The dressing is just superb and the addition of all the crunchy seeds and nuts helps to make this rice salad something really special.

Serves 6 • prep time 15 mins • cook time 45 mins • ½ serve of veg per serve • V • GF

1 cup (185 grams) brown rice
¼ cup light soy sauce or tamari
1 small red onion, finely chopped
3 spring onions, sliced
1 red capsicum, chopped into small cubes
2 medium carrots (1 cup), grated
1 zucchini (½ cup), grated
½ cup pistachios or cashews, toasted
½ cup sunflower seeds, toasted
½ cup pumpkin seeds, toasted
½ cup sesame seeds, toasted
fresh coriander or other herbs, garnish

Dressing

2 tablespoons extra virgin olive oil
2 tablespoons lemon juice
1 teaspoon lemon zest
1 clove garlic, finely chopped
1 teaspoon grated fresh ginger
1 teaspoon honey or maple syrup

1. Place rice and 2 cups of water in a tightly covered saucepan and simmer for 30–45 minutes, until the rice is tender and the water has all been absorbed.
2. When cooked, immediately add the soy sauce and finely chopped red onion to the hot, cooked rice.
3. Mix well, replace the lid and set aside for at least 2 hours, or overnight if you have the time.
4. Meanwhile, make the dressing: Combine all ingredients in a jar with a tight fitting lid and shake well.
5. After its standing time, add the spring onions, capsicum, carrot, zucchini, pistachios or cashews and seeds to the rice and mix well.
6. Toss the dressing through the salad just before serving garnished with fresh herbs.

COOK'S TIPS

When first cooked, long grain rice is low GI, whereas typically medium grain is medium GI and short grain, high GI. However, when cold, they all become low GI. Despite there not being much difference between the GI of brown vs white rice, you are always better off choosing the less-refined, higher fibre option, as it will always be more nutritious.

EACH SERVING PROVIDES
477 calories (2002 kilojoules), 14g protein, 31g fat, 4g saturated fat, 33g carbohydrate and 7g fibre

Veggie salads

Salads are a great way to showcase the season's best produce. Whether raw or cooked, I believe any vegetable can be transformed into an enticing salad. Since most of the following recipes (apart from the Sprouted spring salad) do not contain grains or legumes, I consider them lighter and prefer to serve them as part of a meal, or alongside those salads that contain grains and/or legumes. I do hope you enjoy them.

Super simple kale salad with a few variations

Kale is similar to spinach and silverbeet, but has a thicker, tougher leaf. There are many varieties all of which differ slightly in taste, texture and appearance, but my favourite is the curly kale. It can be eaten raw, but the secret is to chop it finely, rub the dressing into the leaves and allow it to 'marinate' before eating. It is worth this small amount of effort as it is incredibly nutritious and in this salad, very delicious!

Serves 4 • prep time 20 mins • cook time 0 mins • 1 serve of veg per serve • V • GF

- 2–3 tablespoons freshly squeezed lemon juice
- 2–3 tablespoons extra virgin olive oil
- 2–3 teaspoons Dijon mustard
- 2 teaspoon honey
- 2 garlic cloves, finely chopped
- ¼ teaspoon salt
- freshly ground black pepper
- ⅓ cup cashews, roughly chopped, optional
- 1 medium bunch of curly kale (300 grams once stalks are removed)

1. Combine lemon juice, oil, Dijon mustard, honey, garlic, salt, and pepper in a jar with a tight fitting lid. Shake well to combine and set aside.
2. If using, toast the cashews in a frypan with a dash of oil.
3. Remove the tough, centre stem of the kale leaves and set aside to use at another time, or discard. Wash kale well. You may need to use several changes of water to do this. Dry as well as possible.
4. Chop kale leaves finely and place in a serving bowl. Pour dressing over and 'massage' into the kale using your fingers. If using, sprinkle with cashews just before serving.

VARIATIONS

- **Kale, quinoa and almond salad** Add 1½ cups cooked quinoa, 2 cups finely sliced red cabbage, 4 radishes finely sliced, ⅓ cup currants and ½ cup toasted flaked almonds. Make salad as above. Stir through quinoa, cabbage, radishes and currants. Just before serving, sprinkle with almonds.
- **Kale, quinoa, edamame and avocado salad** Add 1½ cups cooked quinoa, 1 cup shelled edamame, 1 roasted red capsicum, peeled and diced, and 1 large ripe avocado, diced. Make salad as above. Just before serving, add quinoa, edamame, red capsicum and avocado. Fold through gently to combine.
- **Kale slaw** (Pictured) To your bunch of finely chopped curly kale, add 2 large carrots, grated, and ¼ small red cabbage, finely sliced. Dress with ¼ cup lemon juice, ¼ cup extra virgin olive oil and 2 tablespoons sweet chilli sauce. Pour over, massage in, then top with ⅓ cup mixed seeds (sunflower, pumpkin, linseeds and chia seeds). Garnish with mint leaves.

EACH SERVING PROVIDES
185 calories (775 kilojoules), 5g protein, 15g fat, 2g saturated fat, 6g carbohydrate and 4g fibre

Carrot, beetroot and mint salad

This easy salad is so colourful and crunchy, and what's more, it's bursting with carotenoids – powerful antioxidants that provide health benefits by decreasing the risk of some forms of cancer, heart disease and macular degeneration. Not many salads get better as they sit, but this one does. I use an electric grater which makes this a really fast salad to make. This is always super-popular at my cooking classes.

Serves 6 as a side • prep time 15 mins • cook time 0 mins • 1 serve of veg per serve • V • GF

2 large (250 grams) carrots
1 large (250 grams) beetroot
⅓ cup fresh mint leaves, chopped
2 tablespoons pumpkin seeds

Dressing

1 tablespoon pomegranate molasses
1 tablespoon balsamic vinegar
2 tablespoons orange juice
1 tablespoon extra virgin olive oil
2 teaspoons honey

1. Grate carrots and beetroot.
2. Combine grated carrot, beetroot and mint leaves in a large bowl.
3. Combine dressing ingredients in a jar with a tight fitting lid and shake well.
4. Pour dressing over salad and allow to sit for at least 30 minutes before serving.
5. When ready to serve, sprinkle with pumpkin seeds.

COOK'S TIPS

- You can use sunflower seeds in place of pumpkin seeds, or half and half.
- For a vegan option, replace honey with maple syrup or brown sugar.
- Do ahead: The salad dressing can be prepared up to 4 days ahead and stored in the fridge. The salad can be made the day before. Keep pumpkin seeds separate until ready to serve.
- Whether you roast, boil or pickle them, grate them raw or juice them, you need to include beetroots in your intake as they are incredibly nutritious. Not only are they rich in folate, the minerals manganese, potassium, copper and magnesium as well as fibre, but the beautiful rich purple colour of beetroot is due to phytonutrients called betalains which have potent antioxidant, anti-inflammatory and anti-cancer effects.
- Carrots are sweet, juicy, delicious and incredibly versatile. They can be eaten raw on their own as a super-healthy snack, cooked, baked, in salads, as a juice, in savoury dishes, as well as sweet cakes, muffins and pancakes. Carrots are well known for their beta-carotene content, an orange-yellow pigment that is converted to vitamin A in the body. Vitamin A is an antioxidant which research suggests may help prevent cancer and protect against eye problems, like macular degeneration, in later life.

EACH SERVING PROVIDES
100 calories (420 kilojoules), 2g protein, 5g fat, <1g saturated fat, 11g carbohydrate and 3g fibre

Julienned summer veggie salad

This salad is perfect for summer and it has everything you want from a salad – a delightful selection of summer produce, it is light, fresh, colourful, crunchy, tangy and delicious. You can chop the vegetables by hand, or use a mandolin or spiraliser as they are much faster and the veggies will be more uniform in size.

Serves 4 as a side • prep time 20 mins • cook time 2 mins • 3½ serves vegetables per serve • V • GF

1 red capsicum, julienned

1 medium zucchini, julienned

1 medium carrot, julienned

1 stick celery, julienned

150 grams snow peas, julienned

150 grams sugar snap peas, topped (optional)

4 radishes, sliced thinly

250 gram punnet grape, pear or cherry tomatoes, cut in half if large

1 small container (100 grams) snow pea sprouts or 1 cup of your own home-produced lentil sprouts

1 bunch coriander, leaves and stalks, finely chopped

1 bunch chives, finely chopped

½ bunch mint, leaves picked and chopped

Dressing

¼ cup freshly squeezed lime juice

¼ cup extra virgin olive oil or macadamia oil

1 tablespoon sweet chilli sauce

½ cup (75 grams) walnuts or pecans, toasted and roughly chopped

1. Place capsicum, zucchini, carrot, celery and snow peas in a large bowl.
2. If using, blanch sugar snap peas in boiling water for 2 minutes, then drain and refresh under cold water to stop the cooking process. Add to the bowl along with the radishes, tomatoes, pea sprouts and fresh herbs.
3. For the dressing: Pour lime juice, oil and sweet chilli sauce into a jar with a tight fitting lid. Shake well to combine.
4. Just before serving, pour dressing over the vegetables and mix well to coat.
5. Serve topped with chopped nuts.

EACH SERVING PROVIDES
335 calories (1406 kilojoules), 8g protein, 26g fat, 3g saturated fat, 14g carbohydrate and 8g fibre

COOK'S TIPS

Although I love extra virgin olive oil, macadamia oil, which is also a monounsaturated oil, is just delicious in this salad. It has a beautiful delicate, slightly nutty flavour which teams well with the fresh, crunchy vegetables, fragrant herbs and lime juice. Choose cold-pressed macadamia oil from local Australian producers in NSW and Queensland.

Sprouted spring salad

Super-quick to make and bursting with nutrients, this is a lovely light, crunchy but filling and satisfying salad. It is a great alternative to the usual green salad that can accompany any meal.

Serves 4 as a side • prep time 15 mins • cook time 0 mins • 2½ serves of veg per serve • V • GF

Dressing
- 3 tablespoons extra virgin olive oil
- juice of 1 lemon (approx 3 tablespoons)
- 1 tablespoon raw honey or maple syrup
- 1 clove garlic, crushed
- ¼ teaspoon salt; pepper to taste

Salad
- 2-3 cups lentil or mixed sprouts (see page 53-55 re sprouting)
- 2-3 radishes, sliced thinly
- 1 small cucumber, halved then sliced
- 1 ripe avocado, chopped
- ½ bunch coriander or 1 bunch chives, chopped
- 4 cups watercress
- nuts (macadamias, pecans) or seeds (sunflower, pumpkin), optional

1. Put dressing ingredients into a glass jar with a tight fitting lid and shake until well combined. Set aside.
2. Rinse and drain sprouts. Transfer to a large salad bowl together with the radishes, cucumber, avocado and coriander or chives.
3. Pour over dressing and toss together gently using a large spoon.
4. Fold the watercress through just before serving and sprinkle with nuts or seeds if using.

COOK'S TIPS
- To turn this salad into a more substantial meal, add beans or chickpeas and nuts (walnuts, macadamias). Feta cheese is also a lovely addition.
- Replace watercress with rocket, mixed salad leaves or baby spinach leaves.
- Do ahead: Wash sprouts, coriander, chives and salad leaves the day before using. Store in a covered colander in the fridge. The salad dressing can be prepared up to 4 days ahead and stored in the fridge.
- Sprouts are a living, enzyme-rich food that are easy to digest, packed with plant protein and essential vitamins. Sprouts are a good source of fibre, B vitamins, vitamin C, beta-carotene, vitamins E, K, calcium, phosphorus and to a lesser extent, iron. Sprouting legumes enhances the bioavailability of certain nutrients (meaning these nutrients may be more easily absorbed) including zinc, iron and calcium.

EACH SERVING PROVIDES
327 calories (1374 kilojoules), 9g protein, 23g fat, 4g saturated fat, 24g carbohydrate and 4g fibre

Mains

Here are four of my favourite spring summer main dishes. They are based around seasonal vegetables and legumes, demonstrating that you can serve refreshing, tasty, interesting mains without meat. Main meals are an important part of our day. It is usually the time when we relax together, catch up and share a meal, so it is important to serve something that everyone will enjoy that includes a balance of protein, fats and carbs as well as plenty of vegetables or salad. The following recipes achieve this balance. I hope you enjoy them.

Raw tomato sauce with zoodles

A delicious, quick sauce to serve on zoodles (which are noodles made from zucchini), or zoodles mixed through pasta, which is what I prefer. It is the perfect light meal on a hot summer evening. I love to top this dish with lots of freshly shaved parmesan cheese, extra basil and loads of toasted pinenuts. Yum!

Makes approx 2½ cups sauce • prep time 30 mins • cook time 0 mins • 3 serves of veg per serve • GF • V

½ cup (30 grams) sundried tomatoes

2 Medjool dates, pitted (30–40 grams when pitted)

½ cup boiling water

420 grams fresh tomatoes (approx 4 medium tomatoes)

1 clove garlic

¼ cup fresh basil leaves, plus extra for garnishing

¼ cup fresh parsley leaves

1 tablespoon extra virgin olive oil

½ teaspoon salt

To serve

zoodles – use at least 1 medium zucchini (150 grams) per person

cooked pasta of choice – use approx 1 cup per person

50 grams approx Parmesan cheese

¼–½ cup toasted pinenuts

extra fresh basil or pesto

salad of choice

EACH SERVING (SAUCE AND 1 ZUCCHINI) PROVIDES
125 calories (524 kilojoules), 4g protein, 6g fat, <1g saturated fat, 12g carbohydrate and 6g fibre

EACH SERVING (SAUCE, 1 ZUCCHINI AND 1 CUP COOKED WHEAT PASTA) PROVIDES
350 calories (1472 kilojoules), 13g protein, 7g fat, <1g saturated fat, 55g carbohydrate and 9g fibre

1. Place sundried tomatoes and pitted dates in a medium bowl. Pour boiling water over and allow to soak for at least 20 minutes. If you are using pasta, put it on to cook now.
2. Place soaked tomatoes, dates and water, fresh tomatoes, garlic, basil, parsley, olive oil and salt into a blender (preferably a high speed blender) and blend for 30 seconds, or until you reach desired smoothness.
3. Pour over zoodles, toss through, then top with parmesan, pinenuts and extra basil.
4. Serve with salad.

COOK'S TIPS

- Do ahead: Soak sundried tomatoes and dates the day before or earlier that day. This can even be done several days ahead and stored in the fridge. This sauce will keep in the fridge for 4 days or freeze for up to 1 month.
- If you don't have a spiral slicer (spiralizer), use a mandolin or vegetable peeler to create long ribbons from the zucchini, then slice thinly.
- For a vegan option, replace parmesan cheese with a vegan cheese or just use extra pinenuts.
- This recipe is gluten free if using a gluten free pasta or no pasta! Note if using gluten free pasta, choose a high fibre one made from legumes (split peas, lentils or beans) rather than rice or corn.
- I love zoodles. They are a great easy way to eat more veggies. However, on their own they will not fill you up for very long. That is why I like to combine them with pasta, which is a low GI carbohydrate food, meaning it will provide a slow release of energy which will help fill you up and keep you feeling full for a good length of time.
- Zoodles can either be served raw, lightly steamed or blanched, or lightly sautéed.

Stir fried veggies with honey, soy and basil tofu

This is a delicious, super-tasty and easy stir fry. Many of my clients worry about using soy and other sauces due to their salt content. I see them as a great way to make veggies taste delicious so you can eat loads of them, and a small amount can go a long way. As long as you aren't drowning your meals in these sauces every night of the week, they are fine to use.

Serves 4 • prep time 10 mins • cook time 10 mins • 4 serves of veg per serve • V • GF

Sauce

1 tablespoon gluten free cornflour
1 tablespoon honey
3 tablespoons tamari
2 tablespoons water

1–2 tablespoons extra virgin olive oil
600g firm or silken pressed tofu, cut into cubes
2 spring onions, sliced
2 cups green or red cabbage, sliced
6 Swiss brown mushrooms, sliced
1 small red capsicum, diced into 2 cm squares
4 medium carrots, sliced
2 large zucchinis halved lengthways and sliced
2 small heads broccoli (400 grams), cut into florets
½ cup Thai basil leaves (or regular basil or coriander), roughly chopped

To serve

pre-cooked noodles, rice or quinoa

1. Start by making the sauce: In a small bowl, mix together cornflour, honey, tamari and water and set aside.
2. Heat wok over medium heat. When hot add a drizzle of oil along with half of the tofu. Cook until tofu browns on both sides, then remove from wok and repeat with the remaining tofu.
3. Place empty wok back onto the stove. Add a little extra oil to the wok along with the spring onions, cabbage and mushrooms. Stir fry for a few minutes, then remove to a large bowl.
4. Add a little more oil to the wok along with capsicum, carrots, zucchini and broccoli and stir fry for 5 minutes, until they start to soften. You may need to add a little water if they start to stick.
5. Add cabbage and mushrooms back to the wok along with the basil leaves and stir through.
6. Transfer to serving bowls on top of noodles, rice or quinoa if using.
7. Add tofu back to the wok along with the sauce, stir through to coat and cool until sauce thickens. Add a little extra water if it becomes too thick. Remove tofu from wok and place on top of the vegetables. Enjoy!

COOK'S TIPS

- For a vegan option, use maple syrup or brown sugar in place of honey.
- Tofu is a lovely light and easy to digest protein food. The perfect addition to a lighter summer stir fry.

EACH SERVING PROVIDES
360 calories (1514 kilojoules), 27g protein, 18g fat, 2g saturated fat, 18g carbohydrate and 13g fibre

Vegetable koftas with tomato and tamarind sauce

This is such a tasty dish and always popular in my cooking classes. It was inspired by a lovely dish I had in a café, but their koftas were deep fried. In my healthier version they are pan-fried. The koftas are really quick to make if you have a food processor. The sauce has a lovely hint of spice and a slight sourness from the tamarind which balances the koftas perfectly.

Makes 40 koftas to serve 4 • prep time 20 mins • cook time 20 mins • 4½ serves of veg per serve • V • GF

Koftas

¼ large (400 grams approx) cabbage, roughly chopped

4 medium (250 grams approx) carrots, roughly chopped

½ cup besan (chickpea) flour

2 teaspoons grated fresh ginger

1 teaspoon salt

1 tablespoon extra virgin olive oil

Tomato sauce

1 tablespoon extra virgin olive oil

1 large brown onion, finely chopped

3 cloves garlic, crushed

1 red chilli, deseeded and chopped

2 teaspoons grated fresh ginger

2 teaspoons ground coriander

1 teaspoon ground cumin

2 x 400 gram tins crushed tomatoes

1–2 tablespoons tamarind purée (see tips)

1 teaspoon sugar

½–1 teaspoon salt, optional

To serve

½ cup fresh coriander, roughly chopped

salad

EACH SERVING PROVIDES
223 calories (935 kilojoules), 7g protein, 10g fat, 1g saturated fat, 21g carbohydrate and 10g fibre

1. Heat oven to 170 degrees and line a baking tray with greaseproof paper.
2. Koftas: Place cabbage and carrot in a food processor and purée until finely chopped. Add besan flour, ginger and salt and process until well combined.
3. Heat a large frying pan over medium heat. Using a large teaspoon, roll kofta mix into small balls, flatten slightly and place on a plate. When pan is hot add a good splash of oil and some koftas and cook for 2–3 minutes, until golden brown. Take care not to burn them. Turn over and cook for 2–3 minutes on the other side.
4. Remove from pan, place on oven tray and place in oven to keep warm while you continue cooking the rest of the mix and make the tomato sauce.
5. Tomato sauce: Heat a large frying pan over medium heat. When hot, add a drizzle of oil and the onion and sauté for 3 minutes. Add garlic, chilli, ginger, coriander and cumin and cook for 3 minutes. Add tomatoes. Use ½ cup water to rinse out tomato tins and add to pan. Bring to the boil, then turn heat down and simmer for 5 minutes.
6. Add the tamarind purée, sugar and salt. Stir through and taste to check seasoning.
7. To serve, pour sauce over the koftas and sprinkle with fresh coriander. Serve with salad.

COOK'S TIPS

- This will keep in the fridge for 3–4 days. I do not recommend freezing the koftas as they go mushy.
- Tamarind purée is available in Asian shops or in the Asian section of the supermarket.

Tomatoey eggplant and lentils on sweetcorn polenta

This is adapted from one of my favourite Ottolenghi recipes where polenta is made from fresh corn rather than the usual cornmeal (dried and ground corn). It is much easier, faster and really delicious! This polenta can be used any time as a side dish in place of mashed potato, it makes a great base for chilli, and of course for this quick eggplant and lentil topping.

Serves 4 • prep time 15 mins • cook time 30 mins • 7 serves of veg per serve • GF

2 tablespoons extra virgin olive oil

1 large or 2 smaller eggplants (500 grams), diced into approx 2 cm squares

1 tablespoon tomato paste

¼ cup white wine

4 large (1 kilogram approx) tomatoes

1 cup vegetable stock

1 teaspoon brown sugar

1 x 400 gram tin brown lentils, drained and rinsed well

1 tablespoon chopped oregano, plus a few extra whole leaves to garnish

600g frozen corn kernels or 4–6 fresh corn cobs, kernels removed

500 ml boiling water

120g Danish feta, crumbled

freshly ground black pepper, to taste

a large handful of baby spinach leaves (50 grams)

1. First make the sauce. Heat a frying pan with a lid over medium heat. When hot add 1 tablespoon of oil and the eggplant. Fry eggplant for 4–5 minutes, until it starts to brown. Add ¼ cup water, turn the heat down and place a lid on the pan and allow the eggplant to 'steam' for 5 minutes, or until softened.
2. Remove lid, add the tomato paste, and cook for 2 minutes on medium heat, then add the wine and cook for another minute. Add the tomatoes, stock, sugar, lentils and oregano, and cook for 10 minutes, without a lid. When cooked, put the lid on to keep warm and set aside.
3. While the eggplant sauce is cooking, make the polenta. Place the corn kernels in a medium-sized saucepan, pour in the boiling water, bring back to the boil, then simmer for 2–3 minutes (or 5–6 minutes if using fresh corn). Drain the kernels, reserving some of the water, and transfer kernels to a food processor. Process corn for a few minutes to break as much of the kernel case as possible. Add a little of the cooking water if the mixture is very stiff.
4. Add the remaining tablespoon of oil, three-quarters of the feta cheese, and pepper. Purée quickly then taste and adjust seasoning if needed.
5. Divide the 'polenta' into shallow bowls, sprinkle with spinach leaves and spoon some warm sauce in the centre. Garnish with remaining feta cheese and reserved uncut oregano leaves. Serve with a salad.

COOK'S TIPS

- Eggplant and lentil sauce can be made up to 5 days ahead and stored in the fridge. It can also be frozen.
- Swap the tinned lentils for ½ cup brown lentils, but increase the cooking time to 20 minutes and add extra vegetable stock as necessary.

EACH SERVING PROVIDES
415 calories (1744 kilojoules), 21g protein, 16g fat, 4g saturated fat, 38g carbohydrate and 15g fibre

Something sweet

The following recipes are for what I describe as 'sometimes' or 'occasional' foods. Yummy extras which can be included as part of a healthy intake, as long as it isn't 'every day'! These are a few of my favourites which are quick, easy, delicious and actually quite healthy.

Mango mousse

A very quick and easy dessert that is beautifully smooth and creamy. Nobody will guess what this is made from! For those who don't like mango, or want some variety, there are a few other variations listed below.

Serves 4 • prep time 15 mins • cook time 0 mins • V • GF

1 large ripe mango (360 grams or 1½ cups flesh)

300 grams silken firm or classic tofu, drained

1 tablespoon maple syrup or honey

zest of 1 lime (approx 2 teaspoons)

To serve

fresh mint leaves, pomegranate seeds or extra mango

1. Remove flesh from mango and chop roughly.
2. Add to the bowl of a food processor and blend until smooth.
3. Add tofu, maple syrup and lime zest and blend until well combined.
4. Divide evenly between 4 serving glasses.
5. Place in the fridge to set for at least 1 hour.
6. Serve garnished with fresh mint leaves and pomegranate seeds or extra mango on top.

VARIATIONS

- **Chocolate mousse**
  Replace mango and lime zest with 100 grams dark (60–70 percent) chocolate, chopped, and ¼ cup soy milk. Place in microwave on full power for approx 30 seconds. Remove and stir until melted. Add to food processor along with tofu and 2 tablespoons of maple syrup. Serve topped with fresh raspberries.

- **Lemon mousse**
  Replace mango and lime zest with zest of 1 lemon and ¼ cup freshly squeezed juice. Serve with fresh blueberries or raspberries.

- **Raspberry mousse**
  Replace mango and lime zest with 1 punnet (200 grams) fresh raspberries. Serve with shavings of dark chocolate.

COOK'S TIPS

- The top of the mousse may discolour as it sits, but this will not affect the taste. Use garnishes to disguise any discolouring!
- Mangoes are an excellent source of vitamin C, beta-carotene (vitamin A precursor), high in fibre, low GI, low in calories and taste delicious!

EACH SERVING PROVIDES
158 calories (662 kilojoules), 10g protein, 5g fat, <1g saturated fat, 17g carbohydrate and 3g fibre

Banana ice cream

Made simply from frozen bananas which are blended until smooth and creamy, this ice cream is so incredibly quick and easy and can be adapted in so many ways. Check out my favourite variations listed below.

Serves 2 • prep time 3 mins plus freezing • cook time 0 mins • V • GF

2 large bananas, peeled, thickly sliced and frozen

1. Place frozen bananas in the bowl of a food processor and blend until smooth and creamy.
2. Scrape the mixture down with a spatula if there are any lumps and blend briefly again.
3. Serve.

VARIATIONS

- **Banana 'caramel' ice cream**
  Place 2 frozen bananas and 2 large pitted and roughly chopped Medjool dates to the bowl of a food processor and process to a smooth consistency. If desired, add a tablespoon of tahini and blend again quickly. Either eat immediately or refreeze, but blend again just before eating.

- **Banana choc chip ice cream**
  Stir through 1/2 cup chocolate chips just prior to serving, or simply sprinkle them on top.

- **Chunky monkey ice cream**
  Combine 2 frozen bananas, 2 tablespoons of your choice of milk and 1 tablespoon natural peanut butter in a food processor and blend until smooth and creamy.

- **Sesame coconut ice cream**
  Make as per chunky monkey ice cream, but use coconut milk and replace the peanut butter with tahini. Add 1 tablespoon of honey if desired.

- **Mixed berry gelato**
  Start by placing the 2 frozen bananas into the food processor bowl and whizz for 1–2 minutes, scraping down the sides as needed, until smooth and creamy. Add 1 1/2 cups frozen raspberries and 1 cup blueberries and blend for 1–2 minutes, again stopping to scrape down sides, until the mix looks creamy. Add 1 or 2 tablespoons berry jam (use fruit only, no added sugar) to taste (black currant is my favourite). Blend again until all ingredients are well combined and the mixture has a lovely gelato texture. Scoop into 4 bowls and top with shaved dark chocolate.

EACH SERVING PROVIDES
107 calories (451 kilojoules), 2g protein, 0g fat, 0g saturated fat, 24g carbohydrate and 3g fibre

Carrot and quinoa cupcakes with tofu cashew 'cream'

My husband's favourite cake is carrot cake, so I initially created this recipe for him. They are delicious, lightly spicy, lovely and moist and a much healthier alternative to the usual.

Makes 14 • prep time 30 mins • cook time 20 mins • V • GF

⅓ cup quinoa, rinsed or 1 cup (150 g) cooked quinoa

¾ cup (90 g) wholemeal flour

½ cup (65 g) ground walnuts, cashews or almonds

½ cup (80 g) dark brown sugar

1½ teaspoons baking powder

1 teaspoon ground cinnamon

½ teaspoon ground ginger

⅛ teaspoon ground cardamom, optional

¼ cup raisins

2 cups (250 g) grated carrot

2 eggs

¼ cup cold pressed macadamia oil or extra virgin olive oil

½ cup apple purée/apple sauce

1 teaspoon pure vanilla extract

Topping

⅓ cup (50 g) unsalted raw cashew nuts

150 grams silken tofu

1 tablespoon (20 g) maple syrup

1 teaspoon of lemon zest

fresh fruit, nuts or seeds to decorate

1. Place uncooked quinoa in a saucepan with water, bring to a gentle simmer and cook for 10–12 minutes, or until almost all the water has been absorbed. Remove from heat, cover and stand for 5 minutes.
2. Preheat oven to 170°C. Line 14 muffin pan holes with paper cups.
3. In a large bowl combine flour, ground walnuts, sugar, baking powder, cinnamon, ginger and cardamom (if using).
4. Stir through raisins, carrot and cooked quinoa.
5. In a smaller bowl, whisk eggs, then add oil, apple sauce and vanilla and mix until well combined.
6. Pour wet egg mix into dry mix and gently fold together until just combined.
7. Scoop cake mix evenly into prepared muffin cases.
8. Bake in the oven for 20–25 minutes, or until a toothpick or skewer inserted into the centre comes out clean.
9. Allow to cool in tin before turning out onto a wire rack.

For the topping

1. Put cashews, tofu, maple syrup and lemon zest in the bowl of a food processor and purée for 1–2 minutes or until lovely and smooth.
2. If too thick, add a tiny bit of lemon juice to make the 'cream' just a little more runny.
3. Refrigerate 'cream' until cakes have cooled and are ready to be iced.
4. Ice cakes then decorate with dried or fresh fruit and nuts.
5. Store leftover iced cakes in the fridge for up to 4 days.

EACH SERVING PROVIDES
Cakes only: 158 calories (665 kilojoules), 4g protein, 9g fat, 1g saturated fat, 22g carbohydrate and 3g fibre
With icing: 189 calories (794 kilojoules), 5g protein, 11g fat, 1g saturated fat, 24g carbohydrate and 3g fibre

COOK'S TIPS

- For a gluten free version, replace wholemeal flour with buckwheat flour plus 1 teaspoon psyllium husks.
- For a vegan version, replace eggs with egg-replacer. See recipe on page 250.

something sweet

Peanut butter and chickpea energy balls

One of the most common requests I get from clients is for a healthy snack and these are one of my fastest and yummiest suggestions. No cooking required and you should have all the ingredients on hand. Just remember to eat them slowly and mindfully.

Makes about 30 • prep time 10 mins • cook time 0 mins • V • GF

- 400 gram tin of chickpeas, drained and rinsed or 1⅓ cups cooked chickpeas
- ½ cup (130 grams) natural peanut butter
- 3-4 tablespoons (90-120 grams) honey
- ¼ teaspoon cinnamon
- 1 teaspoon vanilla extract
- 1 cup (130 grams) whole rolled oats
- ⅓ cup chocolate chips, cranberries or dried apricots, chopped, optional
- ¼ cup shredded coconut, for rolling

1. Place drained chickpeas, peanut butter, honey, cinnamon, vanilla and oats in a food processor and blend until well combined.
2. Carefully mix through chocolate chips, cranberries or apricots by hand or pulse to combine, do not purêe.
3. Place coconut on a plate.
4. Scoop out heaped teaspoons of mix and roll between your palms to form a ball.
5. Roll in coconut. Place in an airtight container and store in the fridge.

COOK'S TIPS

- Replace peanut butter with any other nut butter of choice.
- For a vegan version, replace honey with maple syrup.
- For a nut-free version, replace peanut butter with tahini or any other 100% seed butter.

EACH SERVING PROVIDES
58 calories (246 kilojoules), 2g protein, 3g fat, <1g saturated fat, 6g carbohydrate and 1g fibre

autumn & winter

Roasting vegetables

Roasting is my absolute favourite way to prepare and eat vegetables during the autumn and winter months, and frankly I believe all vegetables taste best when roasted! Roasting highlights each individual vegetable's flavour, making them irresistibly scrumptious and moreish, helping you to eat lots of them, which we all need to do. Best of all, this style of cooking is incredibly easy.

Roasting involves cooking vegetables in an oven, where they are directly exposed to dry heat circulating around them. All seasonal autumn and winter veggies respond well to roasting, the only variance is the time they take until they are done.

Root vegetables roast beautifully, as do brassicas. Roasting these veggies turns them soft and sweet and as they develop a deep colour, or 'caramelise', their flavour intensifies and they become indulgently delicious. In fact, I love when broccoli and cauliflower darken and go crisp around the edges, and once you have tried Brussels sprouts roasted, you will never eat them any other way.

So if you dislike the texture and sometimes blandness that comes with boiling or steaming vegetables, I highly recommend you start roasting them instead. It's sure to become your favourite way to cook veggies too.

Here is the easiest way to roast veggies ....

1. Heat oven to 180–200 degrees C and line baking tray(s) with greaseproof paper to save time washing up later.
2. Cut veggies into roughly even-sized pieces and group according to how long they take to cook.
3. Toss your veggies with extra virgin olive oil, salt and pepper. Add garlic and herbs like thyme or rosemary as you like.
4. Spread evenly over prepared tray(s) – making sure you don't over-crowd or they will 'steam' rather than roast.
5. Wait patiently while they do their thing. Most veggies take 20–40 minutes to cook, with longer times needed for larger-sized pieces.

My 10 favourite ways to use roasted vegetables

- Eat them as they are ... naked!
- Toss them with fresh herbs like parsley, thyme and chives or sprinkle with dukkah
- Toss them with a little sweet chilli sauce, balsamic vinegar, parsley, thyme and chives for a lovely warm roasted veg salad
- Add them to any salad – roasted pumpkin is my favourite for this
- Toss them with wholegrains like quinoa, barley, spelt berries or freekeh along with baby spinach leaves or rocket and fresh herbs for a heartier-style salad
- Spread a wrap with hommus or pesto, fill with roasted veggies, top it off with rocket and some feta or goat's cheese
- Make a roasted veggie soup by blending with stock. Stir through a tin of legumes for a more substantial and filling soup and flavour with fresh herbs
- Toss with beaten eggs and fresh herbs and bake into a frittata, or throw them in an omelette
- Use them to top a pizza, flatbread or socca (chickpea pancake, see page 196)
- Blend into a dip and serve with flatbread.

Eating seasonally autumn/winter

Eating seasonally in autumn and winter will provide you with fresh ingredients containing the best nutrition, flavour and quality. In addition, the fruit and vegetables available will provide you with the appropriate nutrients your body needs at this time of the year.

The transition from summer to autumn brings cooler weather, shorter days and the glory of golden autumnal leaves as nature starts to prepare for its wintery rest. As the temperature drops, your body temperature mechanisms are challenged by the cold. Appetite can increase as the body relies more on food to maintain its temperature and you need a more substantial type of fuel. You need foods which will provide a sustained release of energy as well as generating warmth. The fruit and, in particular, root vegetables available in winter, use of spices, preferred slower cooking styles and heavier meals most people favour at this time of year all support this.

Many winter fruit and vegetables team well with warming herbs and spices (think chilli, ginger, cinnamon and cloves) and are best cooked gently and slowly on the stove. Not only do they taste delicious cooked this way (and meat dishes become soft and delicate after long hours of simmering), but they are easier to digest.

Winter crops have immune boosting power as they contain nutrients that help you better cope against the higher prevalence of colds and flus. Citrus fruit, cabbage, broccoli, pumpkin, sweet potato and spinach are all excellent sources of two key antioxidants:
- Vitamin C, known to help prevent or shorten the duration of common colds and flus
- Beta-carotene, the precursor to vitamin A, which is vital for a healthy respiratory system.

As the days shorten and it gets darker earlier, we get less exposure to the sun. This can lead to a drop in serotonin levels, which can cause depression and food cravings (in particular sugar cravings). Low GI carbohydrate vegetables such as sweet potatoes, yams and pumpkin (technically a semi-starch, also known as winter squash) can help to prevent sugar cravings and boost serotonin levels.

Autumn Foods to include: golden autumnal vegetables like carrots and pumpkin as well as onions, garlic and cabbage. Match with hardier herbs like thyme, rosemary and sage. Use mustard seeds, ginger, cumin, fennel, black pepper and cinnamon to add warmth and spice.
Cooking styles: Slower styles with gentle heat like braising and slow simmering.

Winter Foods to include: more warming and deeply nourishing foods like soups, casseroles, pies, risottos and crumbles. Make the most of root vegetables and hearty grain and bean dishes. Spice up your cooking with warming herbs and spices like chilli, turmeric, ginger, garlic, oregano, thyme, cinnamon and cloves.
Cooking styles: Oven baking, stewing and pressure cooking.

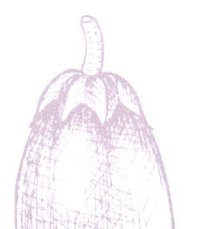  

Autumn season food guide

fruit

- avocado
- apple
- blackberries
- banana
- cumquat
- custard apple
- feijoa
- fig
- grapefruit
- grapes
- guava
- honeydew
- kiwi fruit
- lemon
- lime
- mandarin
- mango
- mangosteen
- nashi
- orange
- papaya
- passionfruit
- peach
- pear
- persimmon
- plum
- pomegranate
- prickly pear
- quince
- rambutan
- raspberries
- rhubarb
- rockmelon
- strawberries
- tamarillo

vegetables

- Asian greens
- avocado
- beans
- beetroot
- broccoli
- Brussels sprouts
- cabbage
- capsicum
- carrot
- cauliflower
- celery
- choko
- corn
- cucumber
- daikon
- eggplant
- fennel
- leek
- lettuce
- mushrooms
- okra
- onion
- onion, spring
- parsnip
- peas
- potato
- pumpkin
- radish
- shallot
- silverbeet
- spinach
- squash
- swede
- sweet potato
- tomato
- turnip
- watercress
- witlof
- zucchini

herbs

- basil
- chervil
- chilli
- chives
- coriander
- dill
- garlic
- ginger
- lime, kaffir (leaves)
- lemongrass
- mint
- oregano
- parsley
- rosemary
- sage
- tarragon
- thyme

Winter season food guide

fruit

- apple
- avocado
- cumquat
- custard apple
- feijoa
- grapefruit
- kiwi fruit
- lemon
- lime
- mandarin
- nashi
- orange
- pear
- persimmon
- pomelo
- quince
- rhubarb
- tamarillo
- tangelo

vegetables

- artichokes—Jerusalem
- Asian greens
- avocado
- beetroot
- broccoli
- broccolini
- beans, broad
- Brussels sprouts
- cabbage
- carrots
- cauliflower
- celeriac
- celery
- chokos
- fennel
- kale
- kohlrabi
- leeks
- lettuce
- mushrooms
- olives
- okra (August)
- onions
- parsnips
- peas
- peas, snow
- potatoes
- pumpkin
- radish
- silverbeet
- spinach
- swede
- sweet potato
- turnips
- witlof (July)

herbs

- ginger
- coriander
- dill
- garlic
- mint
- oregano
- parsley
- rosemary

autumn & winter recipes

Soups
- Pumpkin, leek and red lentil soup
- Lemony lentil soup
- Creamy cannellini bean and kale soup
- Quick minestrone soup

Burgers
- Lentil and cashew burgers
- Mushroom and bean burgers
- Pumpkin, sundried tomato and tofu burgers
- My favourite falafels

Wraps and pizzas
- Black bean enchiladas with kale and guacamole
- Super-speedy kidney bean wraps
- Cauliflower pizza
- Socca with roasted carrots, feta and seeds

Curries
- Quick lentil curry
- Pumpkin and chickpea curry
- Cauliflower and cashew korma curry
- Green curry with tofu

An Indian feast
- Paneer ka salan
- Eggplant with yoghurt and coriander
- Red lentil dhal
- Chickpea crepes

Mains
- Lentil Bolognese
- Baked eggplant with chickpeas and green chilli
- Black bean chilli on soft polenta
- Lentil shepherd's pies

Salads and sides
- Roasted vegetable and barley salad
- Black Beluga lentil salad with baby kale, pumpkin and beetroot
- Carrots roasted with garlic and dukkah
- Chilli and cinnamon roasted Brussels sprouts

Something sweet
- Baked apples with seedy nutty topping
- Rhubarb and walnut crumble
- Apple cake
- Black bean brownie

Soups

There really is nothing better than a steaming hot bowl of soup on a cold winter's day. I love to make soup in large batches and then freeze in individual portions for later. That way, at any time during the colder months I have a selection of soups in my freezer to choose from. Soup makes a great warming lunch or light dinner — plus it is a great way to eat lots of vegetables!

Pumpkin, leek and red lentil soup

This is a great recipe to introduce yourself to lentils. It is also a wonderful recipe for those who say they do not like lentils as you purée the soup so nobody will know they are there! Lentils not only help to thicken this soup, they also add fibre and protein which both help to lower the GI and keep you full for longer. I like to use Jap pumpkin for this soup as it goes really soft when cooked and has a lovely flavour. I also like to leave the skin on the pumpkin. It speeds up preparation time, adds more nutrients and again, as the soup is puréed, nobody will ever know!

Serves 6 • prep time 10 mins • cook time 25 mins • 3 serves of veg per serve • V • GF

1 tablespoon extra virgin olive oil

1 large leek, washed well and finely chopped

2 cloves garlic, crushed

1 teaspoon finely grated fresh ginger

1 teaspoon mild curry powder

1 kg Jap pumpkin, unpeeled, deseeded, roughly cut into 2-cm pieces

1 cup (200 grams) red lentils, rinsed

2 cups (½ litre) vegetable stock

2 cups water

pepper, to taste

To serve

natural or Greek-style yoghurt, optional

fresh coriander leaves

1. Heat a large saucepan over medium heat.
2. When hot, add the oil and the leek and cook for 8 minutes or until soft. If the leek starts to stick or get too brown, just add a little water.
3. Add the garlic, ginger and curry powder and cook for 1–2 minutes.
4. Add the pumpkin, lentils, stock and water.
5. Cover and bring to the boil. Reduce heat to low.
6. Simmer partially covered, for 10–15 minutes or until the pumpkin and lentils are soft.
7. Using a stick blender or food processor, carefully blend until smooth.
8. Season with pepper. Ladle into serving bowls.
9. Top with yoghurt, if using, and coriander to serve.

COOK'S TIPS

- Use organic pumpkin if possible.
- The smaller you cut the pumpkin, the faster it will cook.
- Leeks are in season in winter, but if unavailable, replace with a large brown onion.
- This recipe can be used as a base for other vegetables soups. Simply swap the Jap pumpkin for the same weight of other vegetables such as cauliflower, carrot, zucchini, sweet potato or a mix of vegetables (e.g. celery, carrot and sweet potato).
- Store cold cooked soup in the fridge for up to 5 days or in the freezer for up to 2 months.

EACH SERVING PROVIDES
199 calories (838 kilojoules), 12g protein, 5g fat, 1g saturated fat, 25g carbohydrate and 8g fibre

Lemony lentil soup

I enjoy demonstrating this soup in my cooking classes as it is so quick and easy. The soup is delicious just as it is, but when people add the olive oil and lemon juice on top, I love to watch their faces light up as the flavours are intensified by these additions. This soup is based on the classic Greek lentil soup 'Fakes', but I have added a lot more vegetables. This is sure to become one of your favourites.

Serves 6 • prep time 15 mins • cook time 30 mins • 2½ serves of veg per serve • V • GF

1 tablespoon extra virgin olive oil

1 large brown onion, chopped

4 cloves garlic, crushed

1⅓ cups (270 grams) uncooked brown lentils

8 cups (2 litres) vegetable stock

2 sticks celery (1¼ cups approx, 150 grams), diced

2 carrots (1½ cups approx, 200 grams), diced

1 zucchini, (1 cup approx, 160 grams), diced

1 teaspoon dried oregano

freshly ground black pepper

2 cups (50 grams) baby spinach leaves

To serve

fresh parsley, finely chopped

1–2 tablespoons extra virgin olive oil

juice of 1–2 lemons

1. Heat a large pot over medium heat.
2. When hot, add oil, onion and garlic and sauté until onion becomes soft, 3–4 minutes
3. Meanwhile, rinse lentils and drain well. Add to the pot along with the vegetable stock, celery, carrot, zucchini, oregano and pepper and bring to a boil.
4. Lower heat to a simmer, cover and cook for 20–25 minutes or until lentils are just soft.
5. Place a handful of spinach leaves in the bottom of each of 6 soup bowls.
6. Ladle soup on top, sprinkle with parsley, then drizzle with a little extra olive oil and squeeze plenty of lemon juice over the top. Enjoy!

EACH SERVING PROVIDES
188 calories (788 kilojoules), 12g protein, 4g fat, <1g saturated fat, 22g carbohydrate and 9g fibre

COOK'S TIPS

Store cold cooked soup in the fridge for up to 5 days or in the freezer for up to 2 months.

Creamy cannellini bean and kale soup

Quick, creamy, filling and delicious — need I say more? This is a great wintery soup. And easy to substitute when you don't have precisely these ingredients. For instance, you can swap the cannellini beans for butter beans or even chickpeas. And you can mix and match the vegetables as long as you have a total of 4½ cups before you start cooking.

Serves 4 • prep time 15 mins • cook time 25 mins • 4 serves of veg per serve • V • GF

- 1 tablespoon extra virgin olive oil
- 1 large brown onion, chopped
- 4 cloves garlic, crushed
- 2 sticks celery (1¼ cups approx, 150 grams) diced
- 2 medium carrots (1½ cups approx, 200 grams), diced
- 2 medium zucchini (1¾ cups approx, 200 grams), diced
- 2 x 400 gram tins cannellini beans, drained and rinsed (see tips)
- 4 cups (2 litres) vegetable or chicken stock
- 1 small bunch of kale, stems (and veins, if desired) removed, leaves washed and roughly chopped
- pepper, to taste

To serve
Parmesan cheese (optional)

1. Heat a large pot over medium heat.
2. When hot, add oil and onion, and cook until onion has softened, about 5 minutes.
3. Add garlic, celery, carrots and zucchini and cook for 2 minutes.
4. Add the cannellini beans and stock and bring to a boil, then turn heat down and simmer for 10 minutes.
5. Remove from heat and using a stick blender or a food processor, carefully purée until smooth.
6. Stir in kale and pepper, return to the stove and simmer until the kale is tender, about 8–10 minutes.
7. Ladle soup into bowls and top with Parmesan, if desired.
8. Enjoy!

COOK'S TIPS
- You can replace the tinned cannellini beans with 2⅔ cups or 480 grams cooked cannellini beans or other beans.
- Store cold cooked soup in the fridge for up to 5 days or in the freezer for up to 2 months.
- For a vegan option, sprinkle soup with nutritional yeast in place of Parmesan cheese.

EACH SERVING PROVIDES
215 calories (905 kilojoules), 13g protein, 5g fat, <1g saturated fat, 24g carbohydrate and 13g fibre

Quick minestrone soup

My favourite way to make minestrone is to start with a packet of Italian mixed dried beans, but you have to remember to soak them overnight, plus they take more than an hour to cook. So here's my much faster yet just-as-tasty version. It also includes my secret ingredient — Vegemite — for an Aussie twist!

Serves 8 • prep time 15 mins • cook time 30 mins • 3½ serves of veg per serve • V • GF

- 1 tablespoon extra virgin olive oil
- 1 large brown onion, diced
- 4 cloves garlic, crushed
- 2 teaspoons Madras (or other mild) curry powder
- ½ teaspoon dried oregano
- 3 celery sticks (approx 3 cups), diced
- 4 carrots (approx 3½ cups, 400 grams), diced
- ½ butternut pumpkin (approx 4 cups, 400 grams), skin on, diced
- ½ swede turnip, diced, optional
- 400 gram tin diced tomatoes
- 400 gram tin red kidney beans, drained and rinsed well (see tips)
- 400 gram tin chickpeas, drained and rinsed well (see tips)
- ¼ cabbage, finely chopped (approx 3 cups)
- 8 cups (2 litres) vegetable stock
- 2 teaspoons Vegemite, or more to taste

To serve
fresh basil and/or parsley, chopped

1. Heat a large pot over a medium heat.
2. When hot, add the oil and onion and cook until the onion softens and starts to brown.
3. Add the garlic and cook, stirring for a few minutes, then add the curry powder and oregano and cook for a further minute.
4. Add the celery, carrots, pumpkin, swede turnip, tomatoes, kidney beans, chick peas, cabbage and vegetable stock, then cover with a lid and bring to the boil.
5. Turn heat down and simmer for 15–20 minutes, until vegetables are soft.
6. When cooked, remove a little of the soup liquid and add it to the Vegemite to make a smooth paste. Stir this back through the soup to dissolve completely.
7. Serve topped with basil, parsley or any other fresh herbs.

COOK'S TIPS
- Replace the tin of red kidney beans and tin of chickpeas with 2 tins of 4- or 5-bean mix (or other beans of choice).
- You can replace the tinned beans and chickpeas with 2⅔ cups, 480 grams of any combination of cooked chickpeas, beans and/or lentils.
- Store cold cooked soup in the fridge for up to 5 days or in the freezer for up to 2 months.
- To ensure this recipe is gluten free use GF vegemite.

EACH SERVING PROVIDES
155 calories (653 kilojoules), 7g protein, 4g fat, <1g saturated fat, 19g carbohydrate and 9g fibre

Burgers

Burgers are a fabulous and very tasty way to eat legumes. They are also a quick and adaptable meal, especially if you are cooking for hungry people like young men. Serve them on a bun or in a wrap for a filling lunch or dinner, or with steamed veggies or a salad for a lighter option. I love to team them with a delicious homemade chutney or chilli jam. YUM!

Lentil and cashew burgers

This recipe was recommended to me by one of my lovely clients. It originally came from the Weight Watchers website but I have adapted it slightly adding some curry powder, extra carrots and an egg to help it bind. It has less ingredients than the recipe I used in my café, so is easier and faster to make, but just as tasty.

Makes 8 burgers • prep time 10 mins • cook time 40 mins • 1½ serves of veg per burger

1 tablespoon extra virgin olive oil, plus up to 2 tablespoons extra for frying

⅓ cup (50 grams) raw unsalted cashews, whole and broken

1 large brown onion, chopped

1 clove garlic, crushed

1 teaspoon curry powder

2 medium carrots (1 cup approx, 200 grams), grated

400 gram can lentils, drained and rinsed (see tips)

1 egg

½ cup whole rolled oats

2 tablespoons finely chopped parsley

½ teaspoon salt

finely ground black pepper

1 tablespoon wholemeal plain flour

To serve

⅓ cup relish or tzatziki, optional

winter salad ingredients such as baby spinach leaves or baby kale, avocado, beetroot and carrot

1. Heat a medium sized frying pan over medium heat. When hot, add a drizzle of oil and the cashews and toss around until golden brown. Remove and set aside.
2. Return pan to heat, add the tablespoon of the oil and the onion, cook for 5 minutes or until onion has softened.
3. Add garlic, curry powder and carrot and cook, stirring, for 2 minutes or until softened slightly.
4. Meanwhile, place drained lentils and egg in a food processor and process until puréed.
5. Place lentil mixture, onion mixture, toasted cashews, oats, parsley, salt and pepper in a large bowl. Using your hands, mix well to combine. Using a ⅓ cup measure, shape mixture into eight burgers. Place on a plate.
6. Cover and if you have time, refrigerate for 1–2 hours as they will become more firm and easier to handle. Otherwise continue.
7. Sprinkle the flour on a plate. Coat burgers in flour, shaking off any excess.
8. Heat some of the extra oil in a large frying pan over medium heat. Cook patties for 3–4 minutes each side or until golden and heated through.
9. Serve topped with relish or tzatziki along with a lovely winter salad or serve in a multigrain roll with lettuce, avocado, grated beetroot, grated carrot and relish.

COOK'S TIPS

- You can replace the tinned lentils with 1⅓ cups or 240 grams cooked brown or French green lentils.
- Burgers can be made up to 5 days ahead and stored in the fridge either cooked or uncooked. I do not recommend freezing them. To reheat, microwave for approx 1 minute or reheat in a moderately hot oven for 10–15 mins.
- If you do not purée the lentils, the burgers will not stick together.
- For a vegan version, replace the egg with 1 tablespoon ground linseeds mixed with 3 tablespoons of water.

EACH SERVING PROVIDES
152 calories (638 kilojoules), 5g protein, 9g fat, 1g saturated fat, 11g carbohydrate and 3g fibre

Mushroom and bean burgers

Admittedly these are not the best looking burgers, but they sure make up for that in taste. They are quick and easy to make, will keep in the fridge for up to 5 days (if they don't get eaten first!) and can be frozen (but cook them first). They can also be made smaller and used in place of meatballs with spaghetti and a lovely thick tomato sauce. Enjoy!

Makes 8 burgers • prep time 5 mins • cook time 15 mins • 1 serve veg per burger • V

400 gram tin red kidney beans (see tips)

3 tablespoons extra virgin olive oil

250 grams portabello (approx 3) or Swiss brown (approx 8) mushrooms, sliced

1 medium red onion or small leek, diced

2 cloves garlic

½ cup fresh coriander, chopped

½ cup whole rolled oats

1 tablespoon tamari or light soy sauce

1 teaspoon ground cumin

freshly ground black pepper, to taste

2 tablespoons wholemeal flour

To serve

your favourite relish, chutney or chilli jam, optional

wholegrain burger buns

salad ingredients

1. Drain and rinse the beans, set aside.
2. Heat a medium frying pan over medium heat.
3. When the pan is hot, add a drizzle of oil and the mushrooms and sauté for 4–5 minutes until the mushrooms have caramelised (browned). Then remove from the pan and set aside.
4. Add the onion and garlic to the pan and sauté for 2–3 minutes. You may need to add a little more oil.
5. Remove from heat and add to the bowl of a food processor along with the mushrooms, drained beans, coriander, oats, tamari, cumin and pepper and blend until just combined (about 10 seconds, depending on your blender).
6. Using a $1/3$ cup measure, scoop mixture out.
7. Place on a plate or tray sprinkled with wholemeal flour and toss around to coat, then shape into 8 flattened burgers. Shake off any excess flour.
8. Heat the same frying pan over medium heat, add the remaining oil and the burgers and cook for 2–3 minutes on either side, until browned.
9. Serve with salad and relish or on a wholegrain burger bun with relish, avocado and salad.

EACH SERVING PROVIDES

118 calories (498 kilojoules), 5g protein, 5g fat, <1g saturated fat, 11g carbohydrate and 4g fibre

COOK'S TIPS

- You can replace the tinned kidney beans with 240 grams or $1⅓$ cups of cooked red kidney, adzuki or any other beans.
- Burgers can be made up to 5 days ahead and stored in the fridge either cooked or uncooked.
- Burgers can be frozen but I only do so with cooked burgers.

Pumpkin, semi-dried tomato and tofu burgers

These were a very popular burger I used to make when I had my café. My customers loved that most delicious combination of roasted pumpkin, semi-dried tomatoes and basil. You will find these burgers have a lovely soft texture, with a slight crunch from the walnuts, which are a source of omega 3 fats.

Makes 8 burgers • prep time 15 mins • cook time 40 mins • 1 serve veg per burger • V

- 400 grams Jap pumpkin, skin on, diced small
- 1 tablespoon ground linseeds
- 3 tablespoons water
- 1 tablespoon extra virgin olive oil, plus 2-3 tablespoons extra for frying
- 1 large brown onion, sliced
- 2 cloves garlic, crushed
- 1 teaspoon ground cumin
- 150 grams silken tofu, mashed
- 8 semi-dried tomatoes (30 grams), chopped
- ½ cup (55 grams) walnuts, roughly chopped
- 1 cup whole rolled oats
- 1 tablespoon finely chopped fresh basil
- ¼ teaspoon of salt and finely ground black pepper
- 2 tablespoons wholemeal flour, plus extra as needed

To serve

- ⅓ cup chilli jam or relish, optional
- Winter salad or wholegrain rolls with salad ingredients such as lettuce, avocado, grated beetroot and carrot

EACH SERVING PROVIDES
222 calories (933 kilojoules), 7g protein, 14g fat, 2g saturated fat, 15g carbohydrate and 4g fibre

1. Heat oven to 200 C degrees and line a baking tray with greaseproof paper.
2. Toss pumpkin in a bowl with a drizzle of olive oil. Spread out evenly over the prepared tray and bake for 30 minutes, or until golden brown and soft.
3. Place the ground linseeds and water in a small bowl. Mix well then set aside.
4. Heat a fry pan over medium heat and when hot add a drizzle of oil and the onion and cook for 5 minutes, until softened and starting to brown.
5. Add garlic and cumin and cook for 2 minutes, then remove from heat and set aside.
6. Into a large bowl, add the roasted pumpkin, onion mixture, tofu, semi-dried tomatoes, walnuts, oats, basil, linseed mix, salt and pepper. Mix well, mashing pumpkin slightly.
7. Using a ⅓ cup measure, scoop out mixture and shape into 8 burgers. Toss to coat in flour.
8. When ready to serve, heat a frying pan over medium heat. When hot, add some of the extra oil and cook the burgers until crisp on the outside and warmed through in the middle (3–4 minutes either side).
9. Serve topped with chilli jam or relish along with salad or serve in a wholegrain roll with lettuce, avocado, grated beetroot, carrot and chilli jam or relish.

COOK'S TIPS

- Pumpkin can be roasted up to 4 days before. Store in fridge. Burgers can be made up to 5 days ahead and stored in the fridge either cooked or uncooked. I do not recommend freezing them.
- If you do not have any fresh basil, replace with pesto or any other fresh herb like coriander or parsley.
- The ground linseeds and water can be replaced with 1 beaten egg.
- You can use 150 grams of ricotta in place of the silken tofu.

My favourite falafels

Don't you just love a good falafel? And these are fragrant and delicious, thanks to the abundance of fresh herbs. Falafels are usually made with raw chickpeas that have been soaked overnight, but this is a faster version using tinned chickpeas. However, you will need to rest them in the fridge for 30 minutes to allow them to firm up before cooking. Don't skip this step. Most falafels are deep-fried, but these are pan-fried in olive oil, which is much healthier and less oily. Falafels make a great filling meal when served in a wrap with tahini sauce and salad, but can be served alongside pretty much any salad or vegetables. Make sure you eat them with the tahini sauce, the combination is superb!

Makes approx 20 falafels • prep time 45 mins • cook time • 10 mins • 1/2 a serve of veg per falafel • V • GF

- 2 x 400 gram tins chickpeas (see tips)
- 1 small red onion, chopped
- 4 cloves garlic
- 2 cups (80 grams) fresh coriander, roughly chopped
- ½ cup (20 grams) fresh parsley, chopped
- ¼ cup (10 grams) fresh mint, roughly chopped
- 2 tablespoons ground cumin
- 1 teaspoon sweet paprika
- 1 large red chilli, deveined and deseeded, roughly chopped (optional)
- 1 teaspoon salt
- freshly ground black pepper
- ½ cup sesame seeds
- ½ teaspoon bicarbonate of soda
- 2 generous tablespoons extra virgin olive oil

To serve

tahini sauce, optional — see recipe below

1. Drain and rinse tinned chickpeas.
2. Add chickpeas to the bowl of a food processor along with onion, garlic, fresh herbs, cumin, sweet paprika, chilli (if using), salt and pepper. Blend until well combined.
3. Add ¼ cup of the sesame seeds and the bicarbonate of soda and blend again until well mixed through.
4. Form into approx 20 balls about the size of a walnut, and flatten into discs.
5. Sprinkle remaining ¼ cup of sesame seeds onto a dinner plate and roll falafel around to coat in sesame seeds.
6. Place falafels in fridge to firm up for at least 30 minutes before cooking. If you don't do this, they will fall apart when you try to cook them.
7. When ready to serve, heat a frying pan over medium heat. When hot add some oil and a few falafels (do not over-crowd pan) and cook for 3–4 minutes either side, until golden brown. Repeat with remaining falafels and oil.
8. Serve with tahini sauce.

Tahini sauce

Mix together ½ cup tahini with 1 clove crushed garlic, ¼ cup lemon juice and ¼ cup water (or more for a thinner, runnier sauce).

EACH SERVING PROVIDES

Falafels: 67 calories (280 kilojoules), 3g protein, 4g fat, <1g saturated fat, 4g carbohydrate and 2g fibre
Falafel sauce (serves 20): 41 calories (174 kilojoules), 1g protein, 4g fat, <1g saturated fat, 0g carbohydrate and 1g fibre

COOK'S TIPS

You can replace tinned chickpeas with 2⅔ cups or 480 grams of cooked chickpeas.

Wraps & pizzas

Wraps have taken over from sandwiches here in Australia. I have to admit that it's a trend I love as you can pack a whole lot of interesting fillings inside them — limited only by your imagination!

And next, who doesn't love pizza? The bases I provide here really are a blank canvas on which you can add your own toppings, depending on what you feel like on the day or night! Use these recipes as a guide to get you started, and let your imagination run wild …

Black bean enchiladas with kale and guacamole

An enchilada is basically a corn tortilla wrapped around any type of filling — beans, vegetables, meat, seafood etc. It is then covered with a sauce made from chillies and tomato, and baked. These enchiladas use black beans which are very popular in Mexican food. They are rich in the B vitamin folate, the minerals magnesium, phosphorus and iron, plus they're high in fibre and protein, with virtually no fat. Black beans also contain more antioxidants than most other beans. To reduce preparation time, use a prepared enchilada sauce (basically just tomatoes, onions, capsicum, garlic and cumin) that you will find with the Mexican food in the supermarket, where you also find the corn tortillas.

Serves 4 • prep time 10 mins • cook time 25 mins • 2 serves veg per serve

1 small bunch Tuscan kale, washed

1⅓ cups soft cooked black beans (or a 400 gram tin of black beans, drained and rinsed)

1 large red chilli, deseeded and finely diced, optional

3 spring onions or 1 small red onion, finely chopped

¼ cup (65 grams) Greek yoghurt

⅓ cup (100 grams) ricotta

⅓ cup (40 grams) grated tasty cheese

¼ cup (40 grams) low-fat feta cheese, crumbled or grated

8 small corn tortillas

375 gram jar enchilada sauce

For the guacamole

1 ripe medium avocado, finely diced

juice of ½ lime

salt and pepper to taste

fresh coriander, to serve

To serve

steamed broccoli, green beans or tossed green salad leaves

EACH SERVING PROVIDES
365 calories (1534 kilojoules), 16g protein, 19g fat, 2g saturated fat, 30g carbohydrate and 8g fibre

1. Preheat oven to 180 degrees C. Set aside an 18cm x 28cm baking dish.
2. Cut kale into 3 cm lengths and steam or boil for 6 minutes.
3. Meanwhile, combine black beans, chilli, spring onions, yoghurt, ricotta, tasty cheese and half of the feta cheese in a mixing bowl. When kale is cooked, add and mix through.
4. Warm 3/4 of the enchilada sauce in a large shallow pan over low-medium heat.
5. Use remaining enchilada sauce to lightly coat the bottom of the baking dish.
6. Using your hands or tongs, carefully dip a tortilla in the warmed sauce until both sides are well coated.
7. Transfer the tortilla to the baking dish, scoop in 1/8 of the black bean mixture filling and roll up.
8. Place seam side down in the baking dish, then repeat with other tortillas.
9. When all of the enchiladas have been filled, pour remaining sauce over the top and spread to make sure all parts of the tortillas are evenly coated.
10. Crumble remaining feta cheese over the top and bake for 25 minutes or until brown.
11. While the enchiladas are cooking, gently stir together avocado, lime juice and salt and pepper to taste to make guacamole.
12. Sprinkle baked enchiladas with chopped coriander and top with guacamole to serve.
13. Serve with steamed greens or salad.

Super-speedy kidney bean wraps

This is one of the most popular recipes from my Damn Quick Dinners classes as it is so quick, tasty and adaptable. You can use any beans (black beans are a favourite) or chickpeas, or even a mix of chickpeas and lentils. Here the sauce is used to fill wraps, but it can also be used as a taco filling, on top of nachos or even as a lasagne filling. The options are only limited by your imagination!

Serves 4 • prep time 5 mins • cook time 10 mins • 2 serves of veg per serve bean mix • V

1 tablespoon extra virgin olive oil

1 small red onion, finely chopped

1 clove garlic, crushed

1 chilli, deseeded and sliced, optional

2 teaspoons your choice of spices or spice mixes — Cajun, Moroccan, chilli (e.g. mole poblano) — or simply use 1 teaspoon each of ground cumin and coriander

400 gram tin red kidney beans, drained and rinsed (see tips)

1 x 500 gram jar traditional pasta sauce (or use 1 x 400 gram tin diced tomatoes plus 2 tablespoons tomato paste)

½ cup fresh coriander, roughly chopped

To serve

4 medium tortillas or wraps (high fibre or whole grain)

1 medium ripe avocado, peeled and roughly diced

your choice of salad — carrot, lettuce (shredded) — use whatever you have on hand, sliced or grated

extra salad or steamed greens to serve with wraps

EACH SERVING PROVIDES
321 calories (1350 kilojoules), 9g protein, 16g fat, 3g saturated fat, 31g carbohydrate and 8g fibre

1. Place the oil and onion in a frying pan over medium heat and cook for 3 minutes, or until soft.
2. Add the garlic, chilli and spices and cook for 1–2 minutes.
3. Add the beans and pasta sauce along with a little water you use to rinse out the pasta sauce jar.
4. Stir to combine, reduce the heat and simmer for 4–5 minutes or until thickened slightly.
5. Stir coriander through just before serving.
6. To serve, spoon the bean mixture onto the centre of a tortilla. Top with avocado and salad (as desired), fold over the base and roll tightly. Serve with extra salad or steamed greens on the side.

COOK'S TIPS

- You can replace the tin of red kidney beans with 1⅓ cups (240 grams) of any type of cooked beans you like — black beans, adzuki beans, cannellini beans, black-eyed peas — even chickpeas, lentils or a combination of any of the above.
- This filling can be made up to 5 days ahead and stored in the fridge and can also be frozen for up to 2 months. It gets tastier as it sits!
- Add any type of vegetables you have on hand to this sauce e.g. sliced mushrooms, diced eggplant, zucchini or pumpkin. Include these vegetables when you add the beans and tomatoes, however you may just need to increase the cooking time by 5–10 minutes to make sure the vegetables are cooked.
- This mix makes a most delicious topping for nachos along with avocado and feta cheese or Greek yoghurt.

Cauliflower pizza

This pizza takes quite some time to prepare but is well worth the effort as it is absolutely delicious. The good news is that the base can be made up to 2 days ahead, as long as you have fridge space for storage, then topped and cooked as needed. In this recipe I outline how to make a tomato sauce for the top, but this can be replaced with a jar of pre-made pasta sauce to save on time.

Serves 4 • prep time 20 mins • cook time 55 mins • 6 serves of veg per serve • GF

For the base
- 1 large (950g) cauliflower
- 2 eggs
- ¼ cup (30 grams) fresh grated Parmesan cheese
- salt and pepper

Topping
- 1 tablespoon extra virgin olive oil
- 1 large brown onion, diced
- 2 cloves garlic, crushed
- 1 x 400 gram tin diced tomatoes
- 1 teaspoon dried oregano
- ¼ cup red wine
- large handful baby spinach leaves, wilted in a pan or microwave for 30 seconds
- 2 cups roasted diced pumpkin (400 grams)
- 2 small zucchini (200 gram), sliced and roasted
- 60 grams feta cheese
- 4 tablespoons fresh pesto

To serve
- a lovely wintery salad or steamed broccoli

1. Preheat the oven to 170 degrees C and line two large baking trays (35 x 25 cm) with greaseproof paper.
2. Roughly chop the cauliflower, then place in the bowl of a food processor and pulse until a rice-like texture is created. You may want to do this in at least two batches, depending on the size of your food processor.
3. Transfer cauliflower to a bowl and mix in eggs, Parmesan cheese, a pinch of salt and some pepper.
4. Tip half of the mix onto each of the prepared trays and form into a circle, oval or rectangular shape approx 18 cm in diameter and at least 1 cm thick.
5. Cook for 30 minutes, until bases are firm and start to brown.
6. Meanwhile prepare your toppings.
7. Add a drizzle of oil and the diced onion to a small saucepan and cook over medium heat for 4–5 minutes, stirring all the time, or until onion softens and starts to brown.
8. Add garlic and cook for 2 minutes before adding tinned tomatoes, oregano and red wine.
9. Simmer for 5–6 minutes, then turn off and set aside until base is ready.
10. When the cauliflower base is cooked, spread the tomato sauce evenly over the base, then top with spinach and roasted vegetables.
11. Crumble feta over the top and return to the oven for around 20 minutes.
12. Lastly, dot evenly with pesto before serving.

COOK'S TIPS
- For a slightly firmer base, add 1–2 tablespoons of psyllium husks along with the egg and cheese.
- You can substitute cooked pumpkin and zucchini with any other roasted vegetables such as cooked eggplant or roasted capsicum.

EACH SERVING PROVIDES
287 calories (1205 kilojoules), 16g protein, 17g fat, 5g saturated fat, 11g carbohydrate and 8g fibre

Socca with roasted carrots, feta and seeds

Socca looks like a pizza but the base is actually made from chickpea (also known as besan) flour. It is quick and easy to prepare, high in fibre, low GI and gluten free. As they are filling, I have suggested that each socca serves 2 people with a side of vegetables or salad. You can vary the toppings greatly, but I always include the goat's cheese or feta, seeds and fresh herbs.

Serves 4 (makes 2 soccas) • prep time 30 mins • cook time 10 mins
1½ serves of veg (depending on toppings) • GF

- 1 cup (150 grams) chickpea (besan) flour
- 1 cup (250 ml) soda water
- 2 tablespoons (approx) extra virgin olive oil

Topping

- ½ cup caramelised onions
- 2 cups roasted carrots or other vegetables (see tips)
- 1 cup loosely packed, baby kale or spinach leaves
- 80 grams goat's cheese or feta, crumbled
- 2 tablespoons mixed sunflower and pumpkin seeds, toasted
- ⅓ cup fresh dill and/or other fresh herbs

To serve

steamed green beans or broccoli or a large tossed green salad

1. Sift chickpea flour into a medium sized bowl, add salt and using a whisk, add water slowly to form a smooth batter, then add 1 tablespoon of olive oil. Set aside to rest for 30 minutes while you prepare the topping.
2. Heat oven to 180 degrees C and heat a frying pan over medium heat.
3. When hot, add a good splash of olive oil and half (approx 1 cup) of the batter.
4. Top with caramelised onions, carrots, kale or spinach leaves and goat's or feta cheese and allow to cook for 3–4 minutes, until base is golden brown.
5. Carefully slide the cooked socca out of the frying pan onto a baking tray and bake in the oven for 10 minutes until the top is set.
6. Meanwhile, cook the remaining socca.
7. Before serving, top with a mix of sunflower and pumpkin seeds and garnish with fresh dill or other fresh herbs.
8. Serve with a side of vegetables or salad.

COOK'S TIPS

- You can substitute carrots for roasted pumpkin, cauliflower, eggplant, zucchini, sautéed mushrooms or any combination of these.
- Cooked quinoa is also lovely sprinkled over just after adding the kale or spinach leaves.
- Socca can also be served as a plain flatbread alongside any meal you like. It is delicious cooked on the barbecue too!
- For a vegan option use cashew cheese in place of feta.
- Caramelised onion: Slice one large onion and cook over low heat with 1 tablespoon of oil for 10–15 minutes, stirring regularly, until softened and lightly browned (or caramelised)

EACH SERVING PROVIDES
285 calories (1197 kilojoules), 12g protein, 17g fat, 4g saturated fat, 18g carbohydrate and 6g fibre

Curries

I just love a good curry and there are so many different types to choose from. Curries are definitely one of those meals that benefit with time. The longer they sit, the tastier they become. This gives you a good excuse to make these dishes well ahead of time and even freeze them if you are that well organised. You will be so glad you did!

Quick lentil curry

This is one of my favourite curries as it has a light, fragrant flavour plus it is so quick and easy to make. Feel free to vary the vegetables with what you may have on hand, but I love when you use pumpkin it 'melts' into the sauce and helps to thicken the curry.

Serves 4 • prep time 10 mins • cook time 20 mins • 5½ serves veg per serve • V • GF

- 2 tablespoons extra virgin olive oil
- 1 large brown onion, finely diced
- 2 large cloves garlic, crushed
- 1 tablespoon black mustard seeds
- 2 teaspoons cumin seeds
- 2 teaspoons ground turmeric
- 1½ cups (300 grams) red lentils, rinsed
- 400 gram tin diced tomatoes
- 3 cups vegetable stock
- 1 large or 2 small, 450 grams approx eggplant, diced in 2–3cm squares
- 3 cups (400 grams) Jap pumpkin, diced in 2–3cm squares
- 1 cup green beans, tops removed
- ½–1 cup coconut milk
- 2 cups baby spinach leaves

To serve

- cooked brown rice, barley or quinoa (or wholegrain toast)
- fresh coriander leaves
- Greek yoghurt or toasted cashews
- steamed green beans or broccoli

1. Heat a large pan over medium heat.
2. When hot add the oil, onion and garlic and sauté until onion is soft.
3. Add mustard seeds, cumin seeds and turmeric and cook until the seeds start to pop.
4. Add lentils, tomatoes, stock, eggplant and pumpkin and bring to the boil. Place a lid on the pan, turn the heat down and simmer for 10 minutes.
5. Add green beans, stir through, replace lid and cook for a further 5 minutes or until vegetables are tender and lentils are cooked.
6. When cooked, stir through 1/2 cup coconut milk (or more if the curry is quite thick) and spinach leaves, then turn heat off.
7. Serve on a bed of brown rice, barley, quinoa or a mixture of all three. Top with yoghurt, or toasted cashews (for a vegan version), and fresh coriander leaves.
8. If you are in a hurry and don't have time for the above suggested grains to cook, serve with wholegrain toast.
9. For a lighter meal, omit the grains and serve with steamed green beans or broccoli.

EACH SERVING PROVIDES
416 calories (1747 kilojoules), 25g protein, 13g fat, 3g saturated fat, 45g carbohydrate and 18g fibre

COOK'S TIPS
This curry can be made ahead and kept in the fridge for up to 4 days or can be frozen for up to 1 month.

Pumpkin and chickpea curry

This is a fabulous super-fast and super-easy curry. Pumpkin is such a great winter vegetable and it helps make a most delicious 'gravy' for this curry. It is an excellent source of the nutrients beta-carotene (which our bodies convert into vitamin A) as well as vitamin C. Both are used by the immune system to defend and protect against colds and flus — or help heal if we already have them.

Serves 4 • prep time 10 mins • cook time 25 mins • 4½ serves veg per serve • V • GF

- 1 large brown onion, peeled and diced
- 1 tablespoon extra virgin olive oil
- 2 cloves garlic, crushed
- 1 tablespoon mild curry powder
- 1 cup low-fat coconut milk
- 1 cup vegetable stock
- 400 gram tin diced tomatoes
- 3½ cups (500 grams) pumpkin, skin on, diced in 3 cm squares
- 2 x 400 gram tins chickpeas, drained & rinsed (see tips)
- 2 handfuls (approx 50 grams) baby spinach leaves
- salt and pepper

To serve

- toasted cashews or Greek yoghurt, optional
- ¼ cup roughly chopped coriander leaves
- cooked quinoa, brown rice, pearl barley or other whole grains
- steamed greens such as green beans, silverbeet or roasted Brussels sprouts

1. Heat a large sauté pan over medium heat.
2. When hot, add the onion and olive oil and cook for 5 minutes, or until soft.
3. Add the garlic and cook for 1 minute, then add the curry powder and cook for 2 minutes.
4. Add ¼ cup coconut milk and stir through, then gradually add the remaining coconut milk.
5. Add the vegetable stock, tomatoes and pumpkin and bring to a boil.
6. Turn heat down to a simmer and cook for 10 minutes, stirring occasionally.
7. Add the chickpeas and cook for 5 minutes, until chickpeas have heated through and pumpkin is soft.
8. Add spinach leaves and season as needed.
9. Top with cashews or yoghurt (if using) and garnish liberally with coriander leaves. Serve over a bed of quinoa or other grains alongside a bowl of greens.

EACH SERVING PROVIDES
272 calories (1142 kilojoules), 12g protein, 9g fat, 3g saturated fat, 31g carbohydrate and 10g fibre

COOK'S TIPS

- You can replace the tinned chickpeas with 2⅔ cups (480 grams) cooked chickpeas.
- Green beans (fresh or frozen) can also be added to this curry. Allow around 1 cup or 150 grams.

Cauliflower and cashew korma curry

Please do not be put off by the long list of ingredients in this curry. It is well worth the effort as it has the most amazing flavour. Ground cashews and the selection of spices included make a lovely creamy fragrant sauce that develops in flavour as it sits. Feel free to use other vegetable combinations if cauliflower is not available. Good substitutes are eggplant with green beans or sweet potato with zucchini.

Serves 4 • prep time 10 mins • cook time 25 mins • 3½ serves veg per serve • GF

- 1 large brown onion, sliced
- 1 tablespoon extra virgin olive oil
- 4 cloves garlic, crushed
- 5 cm piece (10 grams) fresh ginger, grated
- 1 tablespoon ground coriander
- 2 teaspoons ground cumin
- 1 teaspoon ground turmeric
- 1 teaspoon ground cinnamon
- 1 teaspoon ground cardamom
- 4 whole cloves
- ½ cup (50 grams) ground cashews
- 2 cups (500 ml) vegetable stock
- 2 cups (500 ml) water
- 1 medium (800 grams) cauliflower, cut into florets
- 1 cup (150 grams) frozen peas
- ½ teaspoon garam masala
- ½ cup natural yoghurt

To serve

- ⅔ cup raw cashews, whole and broken
- fresh coriander
- cooked rice, quinoa, barley or combination of all three

1. Heat a large sauté pan over medium heat and when hot add the onion and olive oil and cook for 5 minutes, until onion softens and starts to brown. Add a little water if needed.
2. Add garlic, ginger, coriander, cumin, turmeric, cinnamon, cardamom and cloves to the pan and cook for 2 minutes, then add the ground cashews and cook for a further few minutes.
3. Slowly add the vegetable stock and water, and mix to make a smooth sauce.
4. Add cauliflower to the pan, bring to the boil, then turn down to simmer for 15 minutes, until cauliflower is cooked through but still firm when pierced with a sharp knife.
5. Add the peas and garam masala and stir through, then add the yoghurt.
6. In a small frying pan, quickly toast the roughly chopped cashews.
7. Turn heat off, transfer to a serving bowl and decorate with toasted cashews and fresh coriander.

To toast cashews

Heat a pan over medium heat, add the raw cashews, a drizzle of oil and cook whilst stirring or shaking the pan for 2–3 minutes until just golden. You should be able to smell the cashew aroma. Take care not to burn.

EACH SERVING PROVIDES
438 calories (1461 kilojoules), 13g protein, 24g fat, 4g saturated fat, 17g carbohydrate and 8g fibre

COOK'S TIPS

- The flavour of this curry really intensifies as it sits.
- For a vegan version, use ½ cup of coconut milk in place of yoghurt.

Green curry with tofu

Everybody seems to love green coconut curries and this is a particularly fine version, if I do say so myself! Make your own paste, it is quick and easy if you have a food processor and will not contain any of the nasty oils they tend to use in commercial pastes. You can also vary your level of chilli this way too, as I find most commercial pastes are too chilli-hot for my palate. Feel free to vary the vegetables you use.

Serves 4 • prep time 20 mins • cook time 30 mins • 4 serves veg per serve • V • GF

- 1 lemongrass stalk, finely chopped
- 2 kaffir lime leaves, deveined and chopped
- 1 bunch coriander, stalks and roots, washed well (reserve leaves for garnish)
- 2 cloves garlic
- 10 grams ginger
- zest from 1 lime
- juice from 1 lime
- ½ teaspoon ground turmeric
- ½ teaspoon ground coriander
- ½ teaspoon ground cumin
- 1 large red chilli, deveined, deseeded and chopped, optional
- 2 cups coconut milk
- 1½ cups vegetable stock
- 400 grams (approx 2½ cups) pumpkin, chopped
- 2 zucchini (220 grams), chopped
- 1 large red capsicum, cut into large chunks
- 1 large head of broccoli (350 grams), cut into florets
- 300 grams firm tofu, cut into 2 cm squares

To serve

cooked rice, quinoa or barley

1. First make the green curry paste: in blender, purée lemongrass, kaffir lime leaves, fresh coriander, garlic, ginger, lime zest and juice, turmeric, coriander, cumin and chilli if using, with ¼ cup coconut milk to make a smooth paste
2. Heat a large pan over medium heat.
3. When hot add the curry paste and sauté for a few minutes.
4. Add remaining coconut milk along with stock. Bring to the boil, add the pumpkin, then turn down to a simmer and cook for 10 minutes.
5. Add the zucchini, red capsicum and broccoli and cook for 5 minutes, until vegetables are starting to soften.
6. Add tofu and gently stir through. Cook for 2–3 minutes, until tofu has heated through.
7. Roughly chop coriander leaves and add to pan.
8. Serve on a bed of rice, quinoa and/or barley.

EACH SERVING PROVIDES
209 calories (880 kilojoules), 17g protein, 9g fat, 4g saturated fat, 11g carbohydrate and 9g fibre

Indian feast

This Indian-style feast evolved as I tried to replicate a dish that we had at one of our favourite Indian restaurants and felt that on its own it didn't constitute a meal. What a perfect excuse to make one of my all-time Indian favourites — dhal — plus cook up a super-fast and tasty eggplant dish and finish off with some delicious crêpes made from chickpea flour to mop it all up with. Enjoy!

Paneer ka salan

This is a delicious dish using paneer, the Indian-style cottage cheese.
You will find paneer in the supermarket in the 'gourmet' cheese section of the fridge.

Serves 4 as part of a buffet • prep time 10 mins • cook time 22 mins • 2 serves veg per serve • GF

- 1 tablespoon extra virgin olive oil
- 1 packet (200 grams) paneer, cut into cubes
- ½ green capsicum, cut into long thin pieces
- 1 red capsicum, cut into long thin pieces
- 1 red chilli, deseeded and chopped
- 3 large spring onions, finely chopped
- 2 cloves garlic
- 1 teaspoon grated fresh ginger
- 1 teaspoon ground coriander
- ½ teaspoon ground cumin
- 400 gram tin crushed tomatoes
- 2 teaspoons tamarind purée (see tips)
- ½ teaspoon salt

To serve
- ¼ cup fresh coriander, chopped

1. Heat a large frying pan over medium heat. When hot, add a drizzle of olive oil and paneer and sauté for 3–4 minutes until the paneer turns golden. Remove from pan and set aside.
2. Add remaining oil, capsicums, chilli and onions to pan and sauté for 3 minutes.
3. Add garlic, ginger, coriander and cumin and cook for 3 minutes.
4. Add tomatoes. Use ½ cup water to rinse out tomato tin and add to pan. Bring to boil, then turn heat down and simmer for 10 minutes.
5. Add paneer back to the pan, along with the tamarind purée and salt, stir through. Turn off heat, but allow to sit for a few minutes before serving to allow the paneer to heat through.
6. Serve sprinkled with fresh coriander.

COOK'S TIPS
- This will keep in the fridge for 3–4 days. I do not recommend freezing.
- Tamarind purée is available in jars in Asian shops or in the Asian section of the supermarket.

EACH SERVING PROVIDES
178 calories (748 kilojoules), 11g protein, 12g fat, 5g saturated fat, 6g carbohydrate and 2g fibre

Eggplant with yoghurt and coriander

This is an amazingly simple way to cook eggplant, yet the result is just delicious. Garam masalas vary greatly in flavour. You can make it yourself, but I really like Herbies (Sydney-based) or Screaming Seeds (Melbourne-based) garam masala blends. The type you choose will make an enormous difference to the flavour of this simple, yet tasty dish.

Serves 4 as part of a buffet • prep time 5 mins • cook time 15 mins • 1½ serves veg per serve • GF

- 1 tablespoon extra virgin olive oil
- 2 medium eggplant (500 grams), chopped into 2 cm cubes
- 3 cloves garlic, crushed
- 2 teaspoons garam masala
- pinch of salt
- ¼ cup Greek yoghurt

To serve
- ½ cup chopped fresh coriander

1. Heat a large frying pan over medium heat. When hot add the oil, then add the eggplant and stir fry for 2–3 minutes.
2. Add the garlic, garam masala and salt and fry for 2 minutes.
3. Place a large lid over the eggplant and allow it to 'steam' over a low heat for about 5 minutes, until the eggplant is cooked through.
4. Turn heat off, then add the yoghurt and mix through.
5. Sprinkle with chopped coriander and serve.

EACH SERVING PROVIDES
82 calories (343 kilojoules), 2g protein, 5g fat, 1g saturated fat, 4g carbohydrate and 3g fibre

COOK'S TIPS
This will keep in the fridge for 3-4 days. I do not recommend freezing.

Red lentil dhal

Red lentils make this dhal super-quick as they only take 10 to 15 minutes to cook. When the lentils are almost cooked, you make a 'tadka' or 'tarka' where spices are tempered in oil in order to release their volatile oils. The tadka is added just before serving and adds the most amazing flavour and aroma to the dhal. Well worth doing.

Serves 4 as part of a buffet • prep time 10 mins • cook time 15 mins • 2+ serves veg per serve • V • GF

1½ cups (300 grams) red lentils

1 large brown onion, finely chopped

1 large tomato, diced

1 teaspoon salt

1 teaspoon turmeric

5 cups boiling water

1½ tablespoons extra virgin olive oil

1 teaspoon cumin seeds

1 teaspoon brown mustard seeds

3 cloves garlic, crushed

½ long red chilli, finely chopped (optional)

a handful (50 grams) baby spinach leaves

To serve

¼ cup fresh coriander, roughly chopped

1. Rinse the lentils and place in a large pot together with the onion, tomato, salt, turmeric and water. Cover with a lid and bring to the boil.
2. Reduce the heat and simmer, half-covered, for 10–15 minutes or until lentils are soft, stirring frequently so that the lentils don't stick to the bottom of the pot.
3. When the lentils are cooked, heat the oil in a frying pan. Add the cumin seeds and brown mustard seeds and fry for about 1 minute until they start to pop.
4. Add the garlic and chilli (if using), removing pan from the heat as soon as the garlic begins to turn light brown. Do not let the garlic burn as it will be bitter.
5. When the dhal is cooked, stir the baby spinach leaves through the cooked lentils, then transfer to a serving dish.
6. Swirl the hot oil mixture over the top and garnish with chopped coriander.

COOK'S TIPS

- If fresh tomatoes are not available, use ¼ cup tomato passata or tinned crushed tomatoes, or omit altogether.
- Turmeric is an amazing spice with strong antioxidant and anti-inflammatory properties. See glossary for more information.

EACH SERVING PROVIDES
300 calories (1263 kilojoules), 20g protein, 9g fat, 1g saturated fat, 32g carbohydrate and 12g fibre

Chickpea crêpes

These crêpes are a quick and easy alternative to the usual roti bread that is served with Indian meals. They are made with chickpea (also known as besan) flour, so are high in fibre and gluten free. Ground linseeds also provide fibre, omega-3 fatty acids and a lovely texture.

Makes 8 • prep time 5 mins • cook time 5 mins • nil veg per serve • V • GF

1 cup (140 grams) chickpea (besan) flour
2 tablespoons ground linseeds
1½ cups water
salt and pepper
2 tablespoons extra virgin olive oil

1. In a medium bowl or 2-cup capacity jug, mix chickpea flour, linseeds, water, a pinch of salt and some pepper together using a whisk to a smooth batter.
2. Set aside for at least 30 minutes to thicken.
3. When ready to cook, heat a frying pan over medium heat.
4. When hot, add a drizzle of oil (just enough oil to coat the pan) and about ¼ cup of the batter mixture and swirl around to cover the bottom of the pan.
5. Cook until brown and crispy, then flip over and cook on the other side for 1–2 minutes.
6. Set aside and keep warm while cooking the remainder of the mixture.

COOK'S TIPS

- This batter can be prepared up to 8 hours ahead and stored in the fridge until ready to use. Any leftover batter can be kept for 24 hours.
- Replace ground linseeds and ¼ cup of the water with 1 medium-sized (67 gram) egg.
- Feel free to double the recipe and make more crêpes. We find them very filling so usually have only one or two each.

EACH SERVING PROVIDES
95 calories (397 kilojoules), 3g protein, 6g fat, <1g saturated fat, 6g carbohydrate and 2g fibre

Mains

These are four of my favourite autumn winter dishes using warming vegetables and legumes. You can serve hearty interesting mains without meat, even in the colder months, and I suspect you will be pleased with how my recipes taste and look. Autumn and winter is the time we crave comforting and warming food and we look forward to sharing a meal with our partners, friends and family. It is important to serve something that everyone will enjoy and these dishes include a balance of protein, fats and carbs as well as plenty of vegetables or salad. I hope you enjoy them as much as I do!

Lentil Bolognese

This Bolognese is a lovely and very tasty alternative to the usual meat-based recipes. Both mushrooms and eggplant, along with either Puy or brown lentils provide a texture and amazing flavour that make it hard to believe it actually is meat-free! I like to serve it on a bed of regular spaghetti mixed with zucchini noodles (zoodles) to keep your serve of pasta to a smaller, more suitable size. Pre-made pasta sauce (simply tomatoes with herbs) is used to reduce the preparation and cooking time.

Serves 4 • prep time 15 mins • cook time 40 mins approx • 5 serves of veg per serve
(or 6 serves if served with 'zoodles', those trendy raw zucchini noodles) • V

- 1 tablespoon extra virgin olive oil
- 1 large or 2 small brown onions, finely chopped
- 1 medium (250 grams) eggplant, finely diced
- 250 grams portabello or other flat mushrooms, finely diced
- 2 medium (200 grams) carrots, finely diced
- 4 cloves garlic
- 1 cup (210 grams) uncooked Puy or brown lentils
- 500 gram jar pasta sauce
- approx ½ cup (125 ml) red wine
- 2 cups (500 ml) vegetable stock
- a handful (50 grams) of baby spinach leaves, optional
- ½ cup fresh basil, roughly chopped
- 250 grams approx wholemeal spaghetti
- 2 medium-large (300 grams) zucchini, optional

To serve

- 1 tablespoon (20 grams) fresh Parmesan, optional
- tossed green salad or green vegetables (I suggest a mix of green beans, broccoli and sugar snap peas)

EACH SERVING PROVIDES

345 calories (1450 kilojoules), 18g protein, 5g fat, <1g saturated fat, 48g carbohydrate and 15g fibre

1. Heat a large sauté pan over medium heat. When hot, add the oil and onion and sauté for 4–5 minutes until it softens and starts to brown. Add a little water as needed.
2. Add the eggplant, mushrooms and carrots and sauté for 3–4 minutes before adding the garlic, and sautéing for a further 2–3 minutes.
3. Add the lentils, pasta sauce, red wine and vegetable stock. Stir well and allow to come to the boil, then turn heat down and if you have a lid, cover the pan.
4. Simmer for 20–30 minutes, stirring occasionally, until the lentils are cooked. Add extra water if needed.
5. Meanwhile cook your spaghetti.
6. While the spaghetti is cooking, shred zucchini into long strips using a spiralizer, mandolin or peeler and knife, so that they look like long thin noodles.
7. When cooked, stir spinach and basil through Bolognese sauce.
8. Just before serving, toss zucchini noodles through cooked spaghetti. Serve Bolognese on top of the 'zoodles' and sprinkle with Parmesan. Serve with salad or vegetables.

COOK'S TIPS

- You can replace the pasta sauce with an 800 gram tin of crushed tomatoes, 1 tablespoon of sugar or honey and 2–3 teaspoons dried oregano, and a pinch of salt or to taste.
- This can be made ahead and kept in the fridge for up to 5 days or can be frozen for up to 1 month.

Baked eggplant with chickpeas and green chilli

This recipe originally came from the Meat Free Week website, contributed by chef Bill Granger. Meat Free Week is a great initiative to raise awareness around the environmental impact of meat production, the effect on our health of eating too much meat and how delicious meat free meals can be! I have changed Bill's recipe slightly, including layering some of the eggplant slices on the top of the dish so they go golden and crispy when baked. YUM!

Serves 4 • prep time 30 mins • cook time 45 mins • 5½ serves of veg per serve • V • GF

3 eggplant (800 grams total), cut lengthways into 1cm-thick slices

½ teaspoon salt, plus 1–2 teaspoons extra

1½ tablespoons extra virgin olive oil

1 large brown onion, finely chopped

3 cloves garlic, crushed

1 tablespoon grated ginger

½ green chilli, finely diced

2 teaspoons sweet paprika

1 teaspoon ground cumin

400 gram tin diced tomatoes

400 gram tin chickpeas, drained and rinsed or 1⅓ cups (240 grams) cooked chickpeas

2 tablespoons pomegranate molasses (see glossary)

freshly ground black pepper

1 teaspoon sumac

1 tablespoon chopped flat-leaf parsley

1 tablespoon chopped mint leaves

To serve

cooked quinoa, optional

salad or steamed beans, broccoli or other winter greens

EACH SERVING PROVIDES
235 calories (986 kilojoules), 7g protein, 9g fat, 1g saturated fat, 26g carbohydrate and 10g fibre

1. Sprinkle the eggplant slices with extra salt, place in a colander and leave for 20 minutes.
2. Meanwhile, heat a frying pan over medium heat. When hot, add a drizzle of olive oil, onion, garlic, ginger, chilli, paprika and cumin, and cook, stirring occasionally, until the onion is translucent, approx 5–6 minutes. Add a little water as necessary.
3. Add the tomatoes along with half a tin of water used to rinse the tin with, chickpeas, pomegranate molasses, salt and freshly ground black pepper. Cook for a few minutes, then turn off and set aside.
4. Turn the oven on to 200°C. Have a casserole dish ready (15 cm x 26 cm and 5 cm deep).
5. Rinse eggplant well to remove the salt and pat dry with paper towel.
6. Place a large frying pan over medium heat.
7. Lightly brush both sides of the eggplant slices with remaining olive oil. Add a single layer to the pan and cook for 3–4 minutes on each side, until golden brown. Set aside and repeat with the remaining slices.
8. Place one third of the eggplant slices in the bottom of the casserole dish. Pour half the tomato mixture over the eggplant slices and cover with another third of the eggplant and then pour over the remaining tomato mixture.
9. Top with the remaining third of the eggplant, then transfer to the oven and bake for 20 minutes. The eggplant top should be brown and crispy.
10. When cooked, sprinkle top with sumac, parsley and mint.
11. Serve with quinoa and steamed greens on the side.

Black bean chilli on soft polenta

Black beans and corn are two foods that just belong together and are a common match in Mexican food. In this recipe, they team incredibly well. You first make a really quick and tasty chilli that is not too hot (and yes, it has chocolate in it!). While it is simmering, you cook the polenta separately and it provides a lovely soft creamy bed for the chilli.

Serves 4 • prep time 20 mins • cook time 30 mins • 5 serves of veg per serve • V • GF

For the chilli

1 large brown onion, diced
1 tablespoon extra virgin olive oil
3 cloves garlic, crushed
2 teaspoons cocoa powder
1 teaspoon dried oregano
1 teaspoon sweet paprika
½ teaspoon cumin
½ teaspoon cinnamon
¼ teaspoon chilli powder
2 medium flat mushrooms, sliced
2 medium carrots, diced
2 medium zucchini, diced
400 gram tin black beans, drained and rinsed (see tips)
400 gram tin diced tomatoes
1 cup vegetable stock
pepper

For the polenta

1 cup cornmeal (polenta)
2 cups vegetable stock
1 cup water
1 cup your milk of choice

To serve

tossed green salad or steamed greens
fresh chilli and coriander
feta cheese, optional

EACH SERVING PROVIDES

316 calories (1329 kilojoules), 14g protein, 7g fat, <2g saturated fat, 47g carbohydrate and 9g fibre

1. Start by making the chilli. Heat a large sautéing pan over medium heat.
2. When hot, add onion and olive oil and sauté for 4–5 minutes, until onion starts to brown.
3. Add garlic, cocoa powder, oregano, paprika, cumin, cinnamon and chilli and sauté for a few minutes.
4. Add mushrooms, carrots, zucchini, black beans, tomatoes and stock and stir to combine.
5. Bring to the boil, then turn down to a simmer and cook for 8–10 minutes, until vegetables are just cooked.
6. Now, while the chilli is cooking, prepare the polenta: place the stock and water in a tall large saucepan over medium heat and bring to the boil.
7. Slowly pour in the polenta while you mix with a wooden spoon to prevent any lumps forming (be careful as the polenta will plop and may spurt onto your hand).
8. Cover the saucepan with a lid, reduce the heat and simmer for 10 minutes, stirring every few minutes.
9. Add the milk and cook for a further 5 minutes with the lid on.
10. To serve, spoon polenta into bowls, top with chilli, coriander and feta cheese (if using).
11. Serve with salad or steamed greens.

COOK'S TIPS

- You can replace the tin of black beans with 1⅓ cups or 240 grams of cooked black beans.
- For the vegan option use soy, almond or coconut milk and replace feta cheese with nutritional yeast or cashew cheese.

Lentil shepherd's pies

A super-tasty version of these popular little pies with a delicious and filling sweet potato top. The smaller you cut the sweet potatoes, the faster they cook — and yes, keep the skin on for extra fibre and nutrients. When mashed, you really cannot tell!

Makes 4 • prep time 15 mins • cook time 30 mins • 5+ serves of veg per serve • V • GF

For the mash topping

600 grams sweet potato, skin on, scrubbed well, diced in 1 cm squares

¼ cup your choice of milk (note — coconut milk is decidedly good in sweet potato mash!)

salt and pepper, to taste

¼ cup freshly grated Parmesan cheese

Filling

1 tablespoon extra virgin olive oil

1 large brown onion, finely diced

3 cloves garlic, crushed

4 medium (100 grams, approx 2 cups) flat mushrooms, sliced

3 tablespoons tomato paste

1 medium carrot (120 grams), finely diced

2 zucchini (150 grams), finely diced

400 gram tin brown lentils, rinsed and drained (see tips)

2 cups vegetable stock

1 tablespoon Worcestershire sauce

1 tablespoon cornflour

1 cup frozen peas

2 tablespoons fresh parsley, chopped

To serve

steamed green vegetables such as broccoli or green beans or English spinach

EACH SERVING PROVIDES
316 calories (1326 kilojoules), 15g protein, 8g fat, 2g saturated fat, 42g carbohydrate and 11g fibre

1. For the mash topping: Cook the sweet potatoes in boiling water for 8-10 minutes, or until very soft. Drain well, transfer to a medium bowl, add milk and salt and pepper to taste and mash.
2. You need 4 individual pie dishes (1¼ cup capacity).
3. Heat a large frying pan over medium heat. When hot, add oil and onion and sauté for 2–3 minutes until soft.
4. Then add garlic, mushrooms and tomato paste and sauté for 3–4 minutes.
5. Add carrot, zucchini, drained lentils, vegetable stock and Worcestershire sauce.
6. Sprinkle cornflour over the top and stir in. Bring mixture to the boil, then simmer for 2 minutes. Turn heat off, then stir through peas and parsley. When cooled a little, taste to check seasoning.
7. To assemble: Heat oven to 200 degrees C. Scoop the lentil mixture evenly into the 4 pie dishes. Top with mash and using a fork, spread evenly over lentil filling to cover but don't flatten them down, give them a rough, rustic, homemade look! Sprinkle with Parmesan cheese and bake for 10–15 minutes or until the top just starts to brown.

COOK'S TIPS

- You can replace the tin of lentils with 1⅓ cups or 240 grams of cooked brown or French green lentils.
- Do ahead — both the filling and the mash topping can be made 2-3 days before using. After preparing, store in the fridge until ready to use.
- For the vegan option, replace Parmesan cheese with 1-2 tablespoons of nutritional yeast or cashew cheese, and check that your Worcestershire sauce is vegetarian.

Salads and sides

The next few recipes are great examples of how, when vegetables are really tasty, you can easily eat loads of them! They are designed to be accompaniments to another more substantial dish, like any of the main dishes in this book or a meaty main such as plain grilled fish or a simple barbecued chicken.

Roasted vegetable and barley salad

This delicious dish came about purely by accident when my husband invited friends for dinner at the last minute and I had to extend the vegetables in our fridge to feed many more than just two. Feel free to vary the vegetables to what you have on hand. I have served this hearty salad as a side to fish and roast chicken but you can team it with pretty much anything.

Serves 6 • prep time 10 mins • cook time 70 mins • 3½ serves veg per serve

1 medium (250 grams) eggplant, cut into about 8 wedges

4 small fennel, each cut into 8 wedges

1 medium or 2 small red onions, cut into wedges

1 medium red capsicum, cut into 2 cm wide strips

1 tablespoon extra virgin olive oil

2 cloves garlic, crushed

¼ teaspoon salt

freshly ground black pepper

4 roma tomatoes, cut in half

½ cup pearl barley

½ cup flat leaf parsley, chopped

¼ cup fennel fronds, chopped

⅓ cup (85 grams) feta

1. Preheat oven to 180 degrees C.
2. Place eggplant, fennel, red onion and capsicum in a large ceramic or Pyrex baking dish (40 x 30 cm, the size you would use for lasagne).
3. Drizzle with olive oil, add garlic, salt and pepper and toss well to coat.
4. Spread vegetables out evenly, then arrange tomatoes on top.
5. Bake in oven for 40 minutes or until browned and vegetables have softened.
6. Meanwhile, cook the barley: Rinse barley then place in a saucepan and cover generously with water.
7. Bring to the boil and cook until soft (25–40 minutes).
8. When barley is cooked, drain and set aside.
9. Remove vegetables from oven, sprinkle cooked barley evenly over the vegetables, followed by the parsley and fennel fronds, then crumble feta over the top.
10. Return to oven and bake for a further 30 minutes, until feta has browned.
11. If the feta starts to brown too quickly, turn the oven down to 160 degrees.
12. Serve hot.

EACH SERVING PROVIDES
165 calories (693 kilojoules), 6g protein, 7g fat, 3g saturated fat, 16g carbohydrate and 6g fibre

Black Beluga lentil salad with baby kale, pumpkin and beetroot

This salad can be served as a light main dish along with some lovely crusty bread, or as a side next to delicious veggie burgers or a frittata. The dressing used here is one of my all-time favourites — it tastes amazing, yet is so simple.

Serves 4 • prep time 15 mins • cook time 40 mins • 4 serves of veg per serve • GF

- 1 generous tablespoon extra virgin olive oil
- 3 cups (450 grams) pumpkin, skin on, diced in 2cm squares
- 2 medium beetroot (400 grams approx), skin on, diced in 2 cm squares
- salt and pepper
- ½ cup (100 grams) black Beluga lentils (see tips)
- 4-5 cups (100 grams) loosely packed baby kale or spinach leaves, washed and dried well
- 1 ripe avocado, optional
- 40 grams feta cheese

Dressing

- 2 tablespoons extra virgin olive oil
- 1 tablespoon balsamic vinegar
- 1 tablespoon pomegranate molasses (see note)

1. Heat oven to 200 degrees Celsius and line a large baking tray with greaseproof paper.
2. Toss pumpkin with a drizzle of oil, a pinch of salt and pepper and place on one half of the prepared tray
3. Repeat this step with the beetroot and arrange on the other half of the baking tray.
4. Bake pumpkin and beetroot in the oven for 30–40 minutes, or until browned and soft.
5. Meanwhile, cook the lentils. Place lentils in a pot with plenty of boiling water and cook for 20 minutes. Drain and set aside to cool slightly.
6. Make the salad dressing: in a small jar with a tight fitting lid, combine the oil, vinegar and molasses and shake well. Set aside.
7. To serve, place the kale or spinach leaves in the base of a large serving bowl.
8. Pour dressing over and toss well to combine.
9. Top with lentils, roasted pumpkin and beetroot, diced avocado, then crumble feta over the top.
10. Serve and devour as it is so delicious!!

COOK'S TIPS

- You can replace black Beluga lentils with French green (Puy) or brown lentils or use a 400 gram tin of precooked lentils, drained and rinsed.
- Baby kale has a much milder flavour than mature kale, making it perfect for salads. If unavailable, use rocket or baby spinach leaves in place.
- Pomegranate molasses is a tangy sweet syrup made by boiling the juice from pomegranates until it becomes thick. It adds a wonderful sour-sweet flavour to your dishes. It is available in most supermarkets. Substitute with 2 teaspoons of brown sugar or honey and 2 teaspoons of lemon juice if you don't have any.

EACH SERVING PROVIDES
440 calories (1848 kilojoules), 14g protein, 28g fat, 6g saturated fat, 29g carbohydrate and 9g fibre

Carrots roasted with garlic and dukkah

I am sure that many people think that eating healthy is boring as it requires you to eat plain steamed or boiled vegetables with nothing on them. This recipe shows just how wrong they are! Extra virgin olive oil as well as the spices, seeds and nuts in dukkah all contain powerful antioxidants. Garlic has antibacterial and anti-cancer properties. All of these add incredible flavours and transform delicious roasted, already incredibly good-for-you carrots, to a whole new level of health. Plus it is so easy!

Serves 4 • prep time 5 mins • cook time 30 mins • 2 serves veg per serve • V • GF

- 5-6 medium sized (600 grams) carrots, unpeeled
- 1 tablespoon extra virgin olive oil
- pepper, to taste
- 1 tablespoon dukkah
- 2 cloves garlic, crushed

1. Heat oven to 180 degrees C and line an oven tray with baking paper.
2. Start by cutting carrots in half lengthways and if large then in half again.
3. Toss in a bowl with olive oil and pepper as desired.
4. Place on prepared tray and bake for 30 minutes, until nearly cooked.
5. Remove from oven.
6. Transfer back to the bowl and toss with dukkah and garlic.
7. Place back on the oven tray and bake for 10 more minutes, until golden and cooked.

COOK'S TIPS
- There is no need to peel the carrots unless they are old and have thick skin.
- Dukkah is available ready made in supermarkets and delis. I have also included a recipe for dukkah in the glossary.

EACH SERVING PROVIDES
101 calories (424 kilojoules), 2g protein, 6g fat, <1g saturated fat, 8g carbohydrate and 5g fibre

Chilli and cinnamon roasted Brussels sprouts

Many people (including me) were fed over-boiled grey Brussels sprouts as children and as a result baulk at the idea of eating them (and let's face it, the smell of them cooking is not so good either!). If you have only ever eaten boiled Brussels sprouts then you need to try these as they taste so different. Roasting Brussels sprouts caramelises the outside, while the insides soften and no sulphur smell is released. Plus you will be nicely surprised by the cinnamon and chilli, which really add a lot of pep.

Serves 4 • prep time 5 mins • cook time 30 mins • 2 serves of veg per serve • V • GF

- 40–48 (600 grams approx) Brussels sprouts (choose the smallest ones you can find)
- 1 generous tablespoon extra virgin olive oil
- 1 teaspoon ground cinnamon
- ½ large red chilli, deseeded and finely chopped, or more to taste
- salt and pepper to taste

1. Preheat oven to 180 degrees C and line an oven tray with baking paper.
2. Trim the ends of the Brussels sprouts, remove any discoloured outer leaves, then cut them in half, or if particularly small, you can keep them whole.
3. Place Brussels sprouts, oil, cinnamon, chilli, salt and pepper in a large bowl.
4. Toss well then spread sprouts evenly over the oven tray.
5. Roast for 30 minutes, tossing halfway through to make sure they cook evenly.
6. When cooked they should be golden brown on the outside, but soft in the centre.
7. Serve as a side, or even as a snack!

EACH SERVING PROVIDES
92 calories (388 kilojoules), 6g protein, 5g fat, <1g saturated fat, 3g carbohydrate and 6g fibre

Something sweet

This book was originally intended to be all about vegetables and legumes, but I decided to include a few of my favourite winter desserts. These are healthier, wholesome desserts with less sugar and fat than the usual, but they still taste decadent and delicious. These foods can definitely be included as part of a well-balanced, healthy intake. It's just a matter of how much and how often.

Baked apples with seedy nut topping

The topping on these apples turns them into something really special.
And it's a quick hot finale for a chilly winter's night meal.

Serves 4 • prep time 10 mins • cook time 34 mins • V

2 large apples (see tips), skin on, cut in half and cored

Seedy nut topping
¼ cup pumpkin seeds
¼ cup sunflower seeds
¼ cup whole rolled oats
1 tablespoon sesame seeds
¼ cup walnuts, roughly broken
¼ cup pure maple syrup

1. Heat oven to 170 degrees C.
2. Place apples in a baking dish cut side down, add 1 tablespoon of water to the bottom of the dish, cover with a lid or foil and bake in oven for 30 minutes. They should be cooked, but still firm.
3. Line a baking tray with greaseproof paper and sprinkle pumpkin seeds, sunflower seeds, oats and sesame seeds evenly over the tray.
4. Bake in the oven for 10 minutes.
5. Remove from the oven, stir to help them cook evenly, add the walnuts and return to the oven for another 10 minutes or until just golden.
6. When cooked, place warm apples in serving dishes, cut side up.
7. Heat maple syrup in a frypan for 20–30 seconds, then add seed, nut and oat mix. Stir until just combined, then remove from heat.
8. Divide topping evenly between apple halves and mound on top using a spoon or your fingers if topping is not too hot.
9. Serve immediately with a scoop of ice cream, yoghurt or custard if desired.

EACH SERVING PROVIDES
296 calories (1244 kilojoules), 7g protein, 16g fat, 2g saturated fat, 31g carbohydrate and 5g fibre

COOK'S TIPS
- This recipe works well with any type of apple, green or red. Or you can replace the apples with pears.
- For a lovely hint of spice, add ¼-½ teaspoon of ground cardamom to the maple syrup.

Rhubarb and walnut crumble

I just love rhubarb and feel it is underutilised as many people don't know how to cook it – yet it is incredibly easy. Despite being eaten like a fruit, rhubarb is a vegetable. It is high in fibre, a great source of vitamin C and potassium, as well as certain phytonutrients which can help prevent cancer. It also contains so little carbohydrate (less than 2 grams per 100 grams), that it is actually not possible to measure its GI. Walnuts not only provide a lovely crunch to this crumble, but are a good plant source of the essential omega 3 fats. This is a gorgeous dessert to serve on a cold winter's night.

Serves 6 • prep time 20 mins • cook time 25 mins • V

- 1 large bunch ripe rhubarb, leaves discarded, stems washed and cut into 3–4 cm pieces
- 2 apples or firm but ripe pears, cored and cut into 1cm slices

Crumble topping

- 3 tablespoons honey
- 2 tablespoons extra virgin olive oil or macadamia oil
- 1 cup whole rolled oats
- ½ cup walnuts, roughly chopped
- ¼ cup desiccated coconut
- 2 tablespoons wholemeal plain or buckwheat flour
- 1 teaspoon ground cinnamon
- ½ teaspoon ground ginger, optional

1. Place sliced rhubarb and apples or pears in a medium sized saucepan with 2 tablespoons of water.
2. Bring to the boil, place lid on, turn heat down to a gentle simmer and cook for 6–8 minutes. When cooked, transfer to a baking dish or ramekins (see cook's tips below).
3. Preheat the oven to 180 degrees C.
4. In a medium sized bowl mix together the honey and oil. If the honey is very thick, warm for approx 20 seconds in a microwave or warm over hot water.
5. Add oats, walnuts, coconut, flour, cinnamon and ginger if using. Stir to combine.
6. Sprinkle crumble topping evenly over stewed fruit.
7. Bake for 15–20 mins for ramekins or 25–30 minutes if using a baking dish, or until golden brown..
8. Serve with custard, yoghurt or cashew cream. You will find a recipe for cashew cream at healthyhomecafe.com.

VARIATIONS

- Use freshly squeezed orange juice in place of water when cooking rhubarb. You can also add a little orange zest or orange peel.
- For a gluten free version, replace rolled oats with rolled quinoa and use buckwheat flour.
- For a vegan version, replace honey with maple syrup.

COOK'S TIPS

- You will need a 2 litre capacity baking dish or 6 x 1-cup oven proof ramekins.
- By including apples or pears when cooking the rhubarb, there is no need to add sugar.

EACH SERVING PROVIDES
277 calories (1162 kilojoules), 5g protein, 16g fat, 2g saturated fat, 27g carbohydrate and 5g fibre

Apple cake

A gorgeously moist, very easy and quick to make cake that is gluten free, low in sugar and high in fibre.

Serves 12 • prep time 10 mins • cook time 50 mins • GF

- 1 x 400 gram tin chickpeas
- ⅔ cup brown sugar
- ¼ cup extra virgin macadamia or olive oil
- ½ cup desiccated coconut
- 1 teaspoon baking powder
- 1 teaspoon cinnamon
- 1 teaspoon vanilla
- 2 eggs
- 2 apples, 1 grated, 1 sliced

1. Heat oven to 170 degrees.
2. Line the base of a 9 inch (23 cm) round cake tin with baking paper and brush the sides with a little oil.
3. Drain and rinse chickpeas. Place in the bowl of a food processor along with sugar and blend until well puréed and smooth.
4. Add oil, coconut, baking powder, cinnamon, vanilla and eggs and blend until just combined, approx 10 seconds.
5. Stir through grated apple by hand, then tip mixture into prepared tin.
6. Smooth top with a knife, then arrange apple slices around the edge of the cake.
7. Bake for 50 minutes or until a skewer poked into the middle comes out clean. Allow to cool before cutting.

VARIATIONS

- Replace coconut with ground almonds or other nuts, or ground sunflower seeds.
- Replace the apple slices for the top of the cake with sliced pear.
- You can make this cake spicier by adding ground ginger, nutmeg, cardamom or cloves.
- You may like to try reducing the sugar further, to around 1/2 cup, and add around 4 large chopped Medjool dates.

EACH SERVING PROVIDES
138 calories (579 kilojoules), 3g protein, 7g fat, 3g saturated fat, 15g carbohydrate and 2g fibre

Black bean brownie

Nobody will believe that there are beans in this brownie – nobody. Black beans are high in fibre, high in antioxidants (polyphenols), low GI and provide these brownies with a gorgeous gooey dark texture. This recipe is so quick and easy you will want to make it again and again. Vary it by adding nuts, or raspberries, and as a dessert option serve with raspberry coulis. Yum!

Makes 16 • prep time 10 mins • cook time 20 mins • GF

- 1 x 400 gram tin black beans, drained or 240 grams cooked black beans
- ½ cup (100 grams) extra virgin olive oil or macadamia oil
- ½ cup (85 grams) brown sugar
- 2 whole eggs
- 2 teaspoons pure vanilla extract
- ½ cup (50 grams) raw cacao powder
- 1 teaspoon baking powder
- ½ teaspoon bicarb soda

1. Preheat oven to 170 degrees C. Line an 8 inch (20 cm) square baking tray with non-stick baking paper.
2. Combine black beans, olive oil and sugar in a food processor bowl and blend until smooth.
3. Add eggs, vanilla, cacao powder, baking powder and bicarb soda, blend again until smooth.
4. Pour the mixture into prepared baking tray.
5. Cook for 20 minutes. Make sure you do not overcook them or they will be cake rather than brownie!
6. Cool before cutting.

To make raspberry coulis

Place 1 cup frozen raspberries and 1 tablespoon pure maple syrup in a glass, ceramic or microwave-proof bowl (not plastic) and heat for 1–2 minutes on high in the microwave. Alternatively, you can heat in a small saucepan on the stove top. Serve warm or cold.

COOK'S TIPS

- Add ½ cup roughly chopped walnuts, pecans, macadamias or any nut of your choice. Sprinkle evenly over the top before baking.
- Raw cacao powder is an unprocessed cocoa powder, so it contains high levels of antioxidants. Other cocoa powders lose most of their healthy qualities when they are processed, which includes treating with heat and sometimes (as in the Dutching process) chemicals as well.

EACH SERVING PROVIDES
89 calories (374 kilojoules), 3g protein, 7g fat, 1.3g saturated fat, 9g carbohydrate and 1g fibre

Glossary

Dukkah

Dukkah is an Egyptian condiment consisting of a mixture of nuts (usually hazelnuts), spices and sometimes herbs. It is typically used as a dip with olive oil and bread or raw vegetables and eaten as an appetiser before a meal.

Dukkah can be used in so many different ways. It is delicious sprinkled onto salads, eggs, added to dips or veggie burgers, sautéed with vegetables, added to roasted vegetables or you can simply top steamed veggies (especially green beans) with Greek yoghurt then sprinkle with dukkah.

It can be varied greatly by changing the nuts used (macadamias work really well) or seeds and adding in different spices and herbs such as fennel seeds, mint or thyme. The name is a colloquial Egyptian word derived from the word 'dakka', which means 'to crush', which is what you do with the ingredients after they have been toasted, which helps to release their flavour. You can buy it ready-made in the supermarket or specialty shops, or make it yourself from scratch which I prefer.

Here is the recipe I use when I make dukkah which comes from taste.com.au

110g (⅔ cup) hazelnuts
80g (½ cup) sesame seeds
2 tablespoons coriander seeds
2 tablespoons cumin seeds
2 teaspoons freshly ground black pepper
½ teaspoon salt

1. Preheat oven to 180°C.
2. Spread the hazelnuts over a baking tray and cook for 10–12 minutes or until toasted.
3. Rub the toasted hazelnuts between a clean tea towel to remove as much skin as possible.
4. Place the toasted and skinned hazelnuts in the bowl of a food processor and pulse until coarsely chopped, or roughly chop with a sharp knife. Transfer to a large bowl.
5. Heat a medium frying pan over medium heat. Add the sesame seeds and cook, stirring, for 3–4 minutes or until golden. Add to the bowl with the hazelnuts.
5. Place coriander seeds and cumin seeds in frying pan over medium heat, and cook, stirring or tossing gently, for 4–5 minutes or until aromatic and seeds begin to pop. Be careful not to let them burn.
6. Transfer spice seeds to a mortar and pestle. Pound until finely crushed (alternatively, use a coffee or spice grinder). Add the crushed spices, pepper and salt to the hazelnut mixture and mix well.
7. Store in an airtight container.

Egg replacer

This is a handy egg replacer for those with an egg allergy, those wanting to avoid eggs, and for vegans. It doesn't work to replace eggs in every type of recipe, but can be used to replace eggs in the burger recipes and pancake recipe in this book.

Vegan egg replacer To replace one egg, mix 1 tablespoon of ground linseeds with 3 tablespoons of water. Mix together, then set aside for 10 mins before adding to recipe.
Note: Chia seeds can be used in place of linseeds.

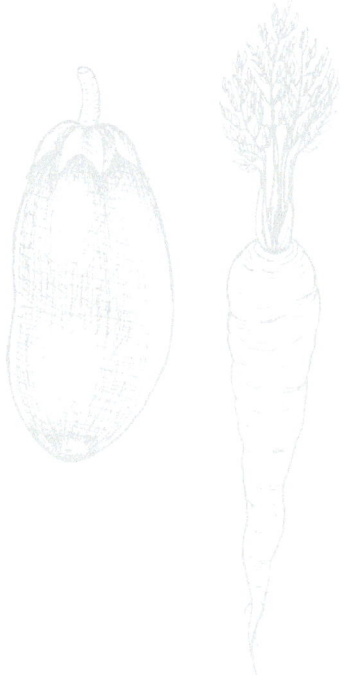

SEEDY CRACKERS

Prep time 20 mins • Cook time 60 mins • V • GF
Makes 50-60

½ cup linseeds (called flaxseeds in America)
½ cup sunflower seeds
½ cup pumpkin seeds
2½ tablespoons chia seeds
2 tablespoons sesame seeds
1 teaspoon psyllium husks, optional
½ teaspoon salt
1 tablespoon extra virgin olive oil
1 cup (250 ml) water

1. Combine linseeds, sunflower, pumpkin, chia, sesame seeds and psyllium husks if using, in a medium bowl. Add salt and mix together.
2. Pour in olive oil and water, mix through, then set aside for at least 15 minutes until the water has been absorbed.
3. Heat oven to 170 degrees.
4. Line a large baking tray (or 2 smaller trays approx 23cm x 32 cm) with greaseproof paper. When the mix is ready, spread evenly over trays using a spatula, approx 3-4 mm thick.
5. Bake in oven for 20 minutes. Remove from oven, transfer to a cutting board and cut into desired cracker sizes. Place back in the oven for a further 20 minutes.
6. Remove from oven again, carefully remove paper, turn the crackers over, then return to the oven for another 10-15 minutes.
7. Cool before eating or transferring to glass jars for storage. YUM!
8. Note: adding psyllium husks makes the crackers a little less crumbly!

Pesto

Basil is at its best in summer, so I love to make pesto and freeze it to use during the year. If freezing, it is best portioned into ice cube trays. When frozen, pop out and place in a container or freezer bag. Pesto can also be stored in the fridge for up to 2 weeks. Here is the recipe I use when making basil pesto. Feel free to double it, depending on the size of your food processor.

1 bunch basil, leaves picked, washed and dried
2 cloves garlic
50 grams Parmesan cheese
⅓ cup (60 grams) toasted nuts such as pinenuts or cashews
⅛ teaspoon salt, optional
¼–⅓ cup extra virgin olive oil

1. Place the basil leaves, garlic, Parmesan, nuts and salt in the bowl of a food processor and process until finely chopped.
2. With the motor running, gradually add the oil in a thin steady stream until well combined and to your desired consistency.
3. Taste to check if it needs more salt.

Pomegranate molasses

Pomegranate molasses is made by crushing pomegranate seeds to obtain the dark reddy purple juice. The juice is then simmered for hours to create a sweet/sour molasses syrup. Great in salad dressings and tomato based dishes. It also makes a great garnish drizzled over food like slow-roasted meats, dips and salads. Available in fruit and vegetable shops or Middle Eastern outlets.

Roasting red capsicums

Red capsicums are at their best and cheapest in summer, so I love to roast and peel them, then freeze them to use throughout the year. Roasted capsicums have a lovely intense, sweet flavour that is a welcome addition to most salads. This is how I roast my capsicums:

1. Preheat oven to 200°C. Place the capsicums on a baking tray lined with greaseproof paper.
2. Roast, turning occasionally, until the skin is charred and blistered.
3. Transfer the capsicums to a bowl and cover with plastic bag or glad wrap.
4. Set aside for 20 minutes, until cool enough to handle.
5. Peel the skin and discard along with seeds. Do not rinse the flesh as it ruins the flavour.

Sumac

Sumac is a reddish-purple spice extracted from sumac berries that grow on a few varieties of Rhus trees. It is used in Middle Eastern cooking to provide a lemony flavour in spice rubs, marinades and dressings. Due to its colour, it is also often used to garnish dishes, especially dips like hummus. Sumac goes well with eggplant, chickpeas and lentils (as well as chicken, fish, seafood and lamb).

A lovely quick tomato relish

Most of the burgers in this book are lovely served with tomato relish. Here is a quick and easy recipe for relish using tinned tomatoes.

Makes approx 6 cups
2 x 400 gram tins diced tomatoes
2 large red onions, diced
1 green cooking apple (such as a Granny Smith), diced
¼ cup apple cider vinegar
2 tablespoons brown sugar
1 tablespoon curry powder
2 teaspoons Dijon mustard
1 teaspoon salt
1 tablespoon cornflour

1. Place all ingredients except cornflour into a large pot over medium-low heat.
2. Bring to the boil, reduce heat to low and simmer for 30–40 minutes, stirring occasionally.
3. Make a paste with cornflour by mixing it with a little water. Stir through relish. Cook for 2–3 minutes, or until mixture thickens.
4. Pour relish into sterilised jars and seal.

Tamari

Tamari is a Japanese style of soy sauce traditionally made from whole soy beans, salt and water (so it is gluten free) and naturally fermented for 2–3 years. I prefer to use it as it is less salty and more flavoursome than most other types of soy sauce.

Tamarind purée

Tamarind is a sticky pulp, extracted from the long brown pods of the tamarind tree. Tamarind is available in many forms in supermarkets in the Asian food section and in any Asian supermarket. I prefer the easy-to-use, ready-to-go purée.

Turmeric

Turmeric is the main ingredient in curry powder. Curcumin, a polyphenol found in the spice turmeric, gives turmeric its golden rich colour. Curcumin is the most potent anti-inflammatory food substance in nature. Its anti-inflammatory properties may decrease swelling and inflammation characteristic of conditions like arthritis, and have been shown to reduce the risk of developing Alzheimer's, dementia and cancer. One teaspoon a day is the recommended dose.

Vegetable stock paste

There are some wonderful stocks now available from supermarkets, delicatessens, gourmet food stores and markets. Admittedly I use these to save on time, however when I can, I make this vegetable stock paste which is just delicious.

It is my favourite quick and easy alternative to using bought stocks. Don't be alarmed at the amount of salt it includes as when mixed with water it is not too salty. This stock paste keeps in the fridge for 2–3 weeks, but I prefer to freeze it in small batches. Because of all the salt it barely solidifies, making it easy to spoon directly from the freezer into your cooking.

Makes roughly 4 jars (approx 3½ cups)

2 leeks (150 g), sliced and washed well
1 small fennel bulb (200 g), roughly chopped
3-4 carrots (200 g), washed and roughly chopped
2 celery stalks (100 g), leaves on, washed and roughly chopped
½ small celeriac (100 g), peeled and roughly chopped, or ½ swede turnip
10 sundried tomatoes (30 g)
3-4 shallots (100 g), peeled
3 medium garlic cloves
½ cup (120 g) salt
½ bunch flat-leaf parsley (60 g), leaves only, roughly chopped
1 small bunch coriander (60 g), loosely chopped

1. Place all ingredients in a food processor and blend to a smooth paste. Depending on the size of your food processor, you may need to do this in batches.
2. Transfer to jars and store in the fridge or freezer.
2. Start by using 1 teaspoon of paste per 1 cup (250 ml) and adjust based on your taste.

Note: While this may seem like a large amount of salt, it is necessary to keep the vegetables from going bad. You are basically preserving the vegetables with the salt. If you use less salt, it is best stored in the freezer. It may be easiest if you use ice trays to do this. Once frozen, cubes can be removed from trays and placed in a bag or other container. Based on a recipe from *The River Cottage Preserves Handbook* by Pam Corbin.

Guide to plant-based protein

Time and time again I get asked if you can get enough protein from plant foods. Yes, you absolutely can! The main thing is to know which plant foods are a good source of protein and make sure you include them regularly. They are:

- legumes — lentils, chickpeas, dried beans, including soy and soy products (tofu, tempeh, milk etc) and split peas
- nuts and seeds
- wholegrains

Then, you just need to be mindful to include these in meals and as many snacks as you can every day.

I have included a chart on the next page that shows how much protein you will get from a typical serve of protein-rich plant foods so you can check for yourself. Record your intake for one day and use this chart to count your protein intake. Here is an example of how to do just that:

SPRING/SUMMER

SAMPLE INTAKE SHOWING PROTEIN CONSUMED OVER A DAY USING LUNCH AND DINNER MEALS FROM THIS BOOK	
Breakfast	
Bircher muesli (recipe at healthyhomecafe.com)	13.0 grams
Lunch	
Chickpea and lentil burger x 2	10.0 grams
with carrot and beetroot salad	2.0 grams
Dinner	
Tofu stir fry	27.0 grams
½ cup quinoa	4.0 grams
Mango mousse	10.0 grams
Snack	
cashews, 30 grams	5.1 grams
1 banana	1.4 grams
small soy latte	5.6 grams
TOTAL DAILY PROTEIN INTAKE	78.1 grams
This is more than the RDI for either a male (64 grams) or female (46 grams)	

PLANT PROTEIN	GRAMS OF PROTEIN PER 100 GRAMS (OR %)	SERVING SIZE AND WEIGHT	AMOUNT OF PROTEIN grams
Lentils, cooked or tinned and drained	6.8	1 cup 198 grams	13.5
Average of all beans, cooked or tinned and drained	8.6	1 cup 170 grams	14.6
Chickpeas, cooked or tinned and drained	6.3	1 cup 200 grams	12.6
Baked beans	4.9	½ cup 140 grams	6.9
Tofu, firm	12.0	1 block 150 grams	18.0
Peanuts, raw	24.7	40 nuts 30 grams	7.4
Peanut butter, natural	28.0	1 tablespoon 25 grams	7.0
Almonds	19.5	25 almonds 30 grams	5.9
Cashews	17.0	20 cashews 30 grams	5.1
Pumpkin seeds	24.4	1 tablespoon 10 grams	2.4
Quinoa, cooked	4.4	1 cup 185 grams	8.1
Barley, cooked	2.9	1 cup 157 grams	4.6
Brown rice, cooked	2.9	1 cup 160 grams	4.6
Soy milk, Bonsoy	4.1	½ cup 125 ml	5.1
Soy milk, Vitasoy Soy milky lite	3.0	½ cup 125 ml	3.8
RDI for adult women 19-70 years			46 grams
RDI for adult men 19-70 years			64 grams

AUTUMN/WINTER

SAMPLE INTAKE SHOWING PROTEIN CONSUMED OVER A DAY USING LUNCH AND DINNER MEALS FROM THIS BOOK	
Breakfast	
½ cup oats cooked into porridge	6.6 grams
with 10 raisins, 5 walnuts and cinnamon	1.5 grams
⅔ cup soy milk	6.9 grams
Lunch	
Pumpkin, leek and red lentil soup (recipe on page 171)	12 grams
1 slice wholegrain bread (Burgen)	4.4 grams
with ¼ avocado	1.0 grams
Dinner	
Lentil Bolognese (recipe on page 221)	7.0 grams
1 cup wholemeal pasta	10.0 grams
Baked apples with seedy nut topping (recipe on page 241)	7.0 grams
Snack	
cashews, 30 grams	5.1 grams
1 banana	1.4 grams
small soy latte	5.6 grams
TOTAL DAILY PROTEIN INTAKE	68.5 grams
This is more than the RDI for either a male (64 grams) or female (46 grams)	

Pantry staples

A well-stocked pantry is essential to help you prepare food quickly. This is my list of the non-perishable items that you will need to make the recipes in this book and are easily available from your local supermarket and/or Asian grocery store. You will then just need to supplement these with the perishable items that you purchase fresh weekly.

Dry goods
- baking powder
- barley
- besan (chickpea) flour
- bicarbonate of soda
- black-eyed peas
- brown rice
- buckwheat flour
- chickpeas
- corn and/or flour tortillas
- cornflour
- cornmeal/polenta
- desiccated coconut
- dry beans: black, butter (or lima), cannellini
- lentils, brown, French green
- nori sheets
- quinoa
- rice paper
- vermicelli (mung bean thread) noodles
- whole rolled oats
- wholemeal plain flour

Tins
- 4 or 5-bean mix
- brown lentils
- beetroot – slices and baby
- black beans
- black-eyed peas
- butter (lima) beans
- cannellini beans
- chickpeas
- coconut milk
- diced tomatoes
- refried beans

Vinegars
- apple cider vinegar
- balsamic vinegar
- (brown) rice vinegar

Oils
- extra virgin olive oil
- macadamia oil, optional
- sesame oil

Jars
- roasted peppers (capsicum)
- sundried tomatoes

Condiments
- Dijon mustard
- dukkah
- enchilada sauce
- horseradish
- light soy sauce or tamari
- miso
- pomegranate molasses
- peanut butter
- red wine
- sweet chilli sauce
- tamarind paste or purée
- tomato pasta sauce
- tomato paste
- tomato relish, optional
- tomato salsa
- Vegemite, optional
- Worcestershire sauce

Nuts and seeds
- nuts: cashews, walnuts, pinenuts
- seeds: sunflower, pumpkin, sesame
- ground linseeds (store in freezer)

Spices
- black mustard seeds
- chilli powder
- cloves
- cumin seeds
- curry powder (mild)
- dried oregano
- garam masala
- ground cardamom
- ground cinnamon
- ground coriander
- ground cumin
- ground turmeric
- sweet paprika

Stock
- good quality vegetable stock

Dried fruit
- Medjool dates
- raisins

Sweeteners
- pure maple syrup
- honey

Note that you do not need to rush out and purchase all of these ingredients immediately. Just stock up on small amounts as you need them and always buy the best quality produce you can afford. I like to buy small amounts of dried legumes, grains, flours, nuts, seeds and spices and buy them often. I also store all my grains, flours, nuts and seeds in the fridge during the warmer months of the year to prevent them from going rancid and limit exposure to pantry moths (I have a separate bar fridge in my pantry for this).

Meal planning

The key to eating well is being prepared.

Plan meals for the week, make a shopping list and you will be ready to go. This helps to avoid food wastage, purchasing unhealthy products and having to visit the supermarket during your time-poor week.

Plan your meals around the seasons to prevent your grocery bill from blowing out and to ensure your meals are full of flavour and nutrition.

On the following pages are two one-month dinner plans, one each for spring/summer and autumn/winter, for you to use as a guide. They include most of the recipes in this book.

I have included 'do ahead' suggestions. If you have a super-busy week, try to **prepare as much as you can on the weekend and store in the fridge or freezer** to reduce time spent in the kitchen during the week.

Also cook in bulk where you **can** so you only need to cook once but get several meals from your effort. You will be so grateful **you** did on those 'heat and serve' nights.

If you would like more information on meal planning, including a meal planning template that you can print and use, go to my website: www.healthyhomecafe.com Click on the 'Eating Well' tab and scroll down to 'How to Eat Well'.

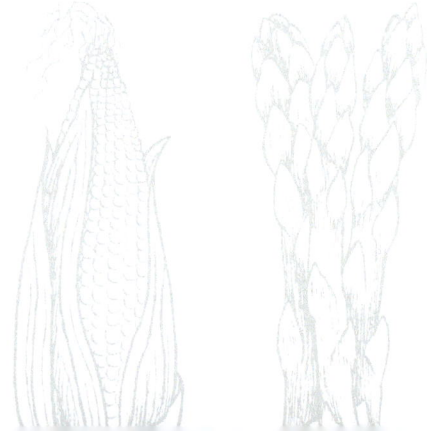

Spring/summer dinner planner

	MONDAY	TUESDAY	WEDNESDAY	THURSDAY	FRIDAY
Week 1	Chickpea and lentil burgers with avocado salsa and Barley and feta salad	Trio of salads: Watercress and lentil; Barley and feta; Black bean and corn	Chickpea and lentil burgers with tomato relish and leftover salad	Vegetable koftas with tomato and tamarind sauce	Dip and crackers; Rice paper rolls with peanut dipping sauce
Week 2	Okonomiyaki with brown rice salad	Trio of salads: Brown rice; Black-eyed pea; Beetroot and lentil	Okonomiyaki with leftover salad	Tofu stir fry	Coconut chapati and bean salad stacks
Week 3	Black bean and quinoa burgers with Carrot and beetroot salad	Trio of salads: Carrot and beetroot; Kale; Potato salad	Black bean and quinoa burgers with leftover salad	Tomatoey eggplant and lentils on sweetcorn polenta	Dip and crackers; Fresh spring rolls
Week 4	Eggplant and adzuki bean burgers with barley and corn salad	Trio of salads: Barley and corn; Sprouted spring; Marinated bean	Eggplant burgers with leftover salad	Raw tomato salad with zoodles and kale slaw	Dip and crackers; Quinoa and brown rice sushi rolls

Do-ahead tips to streamline your weekday dinner preparation:

- **Week One** Make **chickpea and lentil burgers** (Mon and Wed nights); Cook **barley** and dress with dressing (Mon and Tues night); Cook **corn** and make dressing for **black bean and corn salad** (Tues night); Make dressing for **watercress salad** (Tues night); Optional – make **tomato and tamarind sauce** (Thurs night) and freeze.

- **Week Two** Prepare vegetables for **okonomiyaki** (Mon and Wed nights); Make **brown rice salad** (Mon and Tues nights); Cook **black-eyed peas** and dress with dressing (Tues night).

- **Week Three** Make **black bean burgers** (Mon and Wed nights); Make **carrot and beetroot salad** (Mon and Tues nights); Make dressing and wash kale for **kale salad** (Tues night); Cook **potatoes** and dress with dressing for **potato salad** (Tues night); Optional – make **eggplant and lentil sauce** (Thurs night) and freeze.

- **Week Four** Make **eggplant burgers** (Mon and Wed nights); Cook **barley** and dress with miso dressing (Mon and Tues nights); Make dressing for **sprout salad** (Tues night); Soak sundried tomatoes and dates for **tomato sauce** (Thurs night); Make dressing for **kale slaw** (Thurs night).

- **Note** I have assumed tinned legumes are to be used, however if (like me) you prefer to cook all of your own legumes, you will need to add this to your prep list.

Autumn/winter dinner planner

	MONDAY	TUESDAY	WEDNESDAY	THURSDAY	FRIDAY
Week 1	Baked eggplant with chickpeas and green chilli	Cauliflower and cashew korma on barley	Quick minestrone soup	Lentil Bolognese	A quick Indian feast
Week 2	Black bean chilli on soft polenta	Lemony lentil soup	Mushroom and bean burgers	Pumpkin and chickpea curry	Socca
Week 3	Quick lentil curry	Pumpkin and tofu burgers with salad or vegetables	Bean wraps	Lentil shepherd's pies	Falafels
Week 4	Black bean enchiladas with kale and guacamole	Green curry with tofu	Lentil burgers with salad or vegetables	Creamy cannellini bean and kale soup	Cauliflower pizza

Do-ahead tips to streamline your dinner preparation:

- Cook Monday night's dinner on the weekend and store in the fridge.

- Cook Thursday night's dinner on the weekend and freeze. Tuesday and Wednesday nights meals can also be made ahead and stored in the fridge (all of these dishes will keep for up to 4 days).

- Cauliflower pizza base on week 4 can be made on the Wednesday or Thursday night before.

- Cook the minestrone and lentil soups in large batches and freeze. Frozen soups make a great quick and easy lunch.

- Make extra on any night and use leftovers for lunches.

veggie-licious 265

About the nutritional information

I have included a nutritional breakdown with each recipe, intended to be used as a guide only as I don't want there to be much of a focus on the numbers. Counting calories is not the right emphasis for your intake and I don't want you to think that you should be focusing on it either.

Measuring of nutrients isn't always precise and these numbers are only relevant if you measure the ingredients in the recipes accurately and eat the correct serving size too! Everyone has different energy levels, appetites and energy needs. Please bear this in mind when considering the serving sizes I have suggested and adjust the portions accordingly for your requirements.

The information provided includes a guide for energy, which is measured in both calories and kilojoules, as well as protein, total fat and saturated fat, carbohydrate and fibre per serving. These numbers are a guide which can be useful for those with diabetes, insulin resistance, those who must be extra careful with their fat intake and for anyone tracking their fibre intake. Other nutrition guides I have included are:
- vegan — for those who avoid all products that come from an animal, including dairy and honey
- gluten free — for those with coeliac disease or those with gluten intolerance

To guarantee these recipes are strictly gluten free, you will need to check that ingredients such as stock, sauces like tamari or soy sauce, yoghurt and cornflour are all gluten free. Some of the other recipes can also become gluten free if you swap oats for gluten free breadcrumbs or quinoa flakes, and use gluten free pasta.

All of the recipes included are low in saturated fat, low GI and high in fibre.

A note about salt

Salt (a compound made from sodium and chloride) is used to both preserve and flavour food. A small amount is necessary for good health as it is required for fluid balance in the body and proper muscle and nerve function. The kidneys regulate your sodium levels.

A high intake of salt is associated with high blood pressure, fluid retention and other medical conditions. It therefore should be added mindfully and in moderation. However, unless you are under doctor's orders to restrict your use of salt, you should not be afraid to season your food as healthy food should not taste dull or boring. Besides, 75 percent of a person's salt intake in a typical Australian diet comes from processed foods, packaged foods and take away foods. Reducing these foods will have a greater effect on keeping your salt intake low.

Any clients who come and see me to help lower their high blood pressure get introduced to the DASH diet — a dietary approach which has been shown to reduce hypertension (high blood pressure). In this approach foods high in potassium (and magnesium) are successfully used to offset the effects of sodium. All plant food, including vegetables and legumes, are high in both potassium and magnesium and naturally low in sodium. I have seen an increase in plant based foods reduce high blood pressure in many of my clients, even when they still add a little salt to their cooking.

References and conversion charts

B. Dawson-Hughes, S. S. Harris, L. Ceglia. *Alkaline diets favor lean tissue mass in older adults.* Am. J. Clin. Nutr. 2008 87(3):662 – 665.

http://cancerpreventionresearch.aacrjournals.org/content/4/2/177.short

Is a vegetarian diet adequate? *Medical Journal of Australia Supplement* Available at www.mja.com.au/open/2012/1/2

www.eatforhealth.gov.au
www.nrv.gov.au
www.healthyhomecafe.com

Hot pots and extra virgin olive oil – do they mix? https://www.australianolives.com.au/assets/files/pdfs/aoa-forms/Media%20Releases/MR%20-%202011%20-%20Smoke%20point%20oils.pdf

Solids

METRIC	IMPERIAL
20 grams	½ oz
60 grams	2 oz
125 grams	4 oz
180 grams	6 oz
250 grams	8 oz
500 grams	16 oz (1lb)
1 kilogram	32 oz (2lb)

Australian metric cup and spoon measures

CUP	METRIC	IMPERIAL — LIQUIDS
¼	60ml	2 fl oz
⅓	80ml	2½ fl oz
½	125ml	4 fl oz
1 cup	250ml	8 fl oz

SPOON	METRIC
¼ teaspoon	1.25 ml
½ teaspoon	2.5 ml
1 teaspoon	5 ml
1 tablespoon (4 teaspoons)*	20 ml

*Note: North America, New Zealand and the United Kingdom use a 15ml tablespoon

Oven temperatures

	°CELSIUS	°FAHRENHEIT	FAN-FORCED OVENS
Very slow	120	250	If using a fan-forced oven, decrease the temperature by 10–20 degrees
Slow	150	300	
Moderately slow	160	325	
Moderate	180	350	
Moderately hot	190	175	
Hot	200	400	
Very hot	220–250	450–500	

'One cannot think well, love well, sleep well,
if one has not dined well.'

Virginia Woolf

About Caroline Trickey

APD, B Sc, Nutr and Dietetics Monash University

Caroline Trickey is a qualified dietitian and nutritionist who works in private practice and runs a cooking school and blog called Healthy Home Café.

The cooking school is designed to show people how to cook delicious, nutritious food quickly and easily. During the classes, Caroline teaches how food can boost your energy, reduce inflammation (inflammation can encourage weight gain, heart disease, cancer, and worsen symptoms from auto-immune conditions) and get more plant-based foods into your intake, a very healthy thing to do!

In a past life, Caroline ran a successful café and catering business. She has a true love and passion for cooking and wants to show people that food is there to nourish us, for enjoyment and pleasure.

Caroline believes in a healthy balance and avoids diets and shaming foods (i.e. she enjoys all food and bakes a mean cake!). Rather she has a more sensible, practical and balanced approach — one that really works long term!

You can access more than 300 of her delicious recipes and find out more about her cooking classes on her website: www.healthyhomecafe.com

Index

A
adzuki beans 39, 40
   cooking 40, 43
   eggplant and adzuki bean burgers 80
ageing 17
ALA (alpha-linolenic acid) 20
alfalfa 54
allergies 13, 14
allicin 17
almonds 13
   kale, quinoa and almond salad 129
   nutrient composition 24
Alzheimer's 15, 17
amino acids 21
anthocyanins 17
antioxidants 10, 14, 25
apples 17
   apple cake 245
   baked apples with seedy nutty topping 241
   rhubarb and walnut crumble 242
apricots 17
arthritis 14
artichokes 13
asthma 13, 14
auto-immune conditions 14, 20
autumn
   meal planner 265
   plant-based protein guide 258
   recipes 167
   seasonal food guide 163, 164
avocado
   black bean salad with corn and avocado 103
   coconut chapati, bean and salad stacks 89
   Greek salad with avocado and chickpeas 113
   green goddess slaw with chickpeas 114
   guacamole 191
   kale, quinoa, edamame and avocado salad 129
   salsa 83
   sprouted spring salad 134
   summertime rice paper rolls with peanut dipping sauce 93

B
bacteria 12, 13
baked apples with seedy nutty topping 241
baked eggplant with chickpeas and green chilli 222
bananas 13, 22
   banana 'caramel' ice cream 150
   banana choc chip ice cream 150
   ice cream 150
barley 12, 13, 19, 47
   barley and corn salad with miso dressing 120
   barley salad with tomatoes, feta and basil 119
   cooking 47
   nutrient composition 24
   roasted vegetable and barley salad 231
basil
   barley salad with tomatoes, feta and basil 119
   basil-pesto hommus 69
   pesto 253
   semi-dried tomato and basil hommus 69
   stir fried veggies with honey, soy and basil tofu 140
beans 19, 37–43 *see also by type*
   cooking 37, 40, 43
   dried 13, 22, 37
   marinated bean salad 99
   nutrient composition 24
   salads 65, 97
   tinned 37
beef 20
beetroot 19
   beetroot, lentil, feta and walnut salad 109
   black Beluga lentil salad with baby kale, pumpkin and beetroot 232
   carrot and beetroot salad 130
   coconut chapati, bean and salad stacks 89
   dip 70
beta-carotene 17, 163
bioflavanoids 17
black beans 38, 39
   black bean brownie 246
   black bean chilli on soft polenta 225
   black bean enchiladas with kale and guacamole 191
   black bean and mango salad 103
   black bean and quinoa burgers 79
   black bean salad with corn and avocado 103
   cooking 38, 43
   black Beluga lentil salad with baby kale, pumpkin and beetroot 232
black-eyed peas 39, 40
black-eyed peas with garlic and lemon 100
   cooking 40, 43
blackberries 17
blackcurrants 17
blood pressure 14, 17
blood sugar levels 19
blueberries 17
   mixed berry gelato 150
borlotti beans 38
   cooking 38, 43
bread 19
broccoli 15, 17
   quinoa, lentil and broccoli salad 123
   stir fried veggies with honey, soy and basil tofu 140
brown rice salad 124
Brussels sprouts 17, 20
   chilli and cinnamon roasted Brussels sprouts 236
buckwheat 47, 54
   cooking 47
burgers 65, 77, 167, 179
   black bean and quinoa 79
   chickpea and lentil with avocado salsa 83
   eggplant and adzuki bean 80
   lentil and cashew 181
   mushroom and bean 182
   my favourite falafels 186
   pumpkin, semi-dried tomato and tofu 185
butter beans *see* Lima (butter) beans

C
cabbage 17
   green goddess slaw with chickpeas 114
   okonomiyaki (Japanese pancake) 84
   quick minestrone 176
   stir fried veggies with honey, soy and basil tofu 140
   vegetable koftas with tomato and tamarind sauce 143
cakes
   apple cake 245
   black bean brownie 246
cancer 12, 15, 17, 19, 22
cannellini beans 24, 38, 39
   cooking 38, 43
   creamy cannellini bean and kale soup 175
   white bean aioli 74
   white bean and basil dip 74

white bean dip with garlic and herbs 74
capsicum
   fresh spring rolls 90
   julienned summer veggie salad 133
   muhumarra 73
   okonomiyaki (Japanese pancake) 84
   paneer ka salan 211
   roasted capsicum hommus 69
   roasting red capsicums 253
   summertime rice paper rolls with peanut dipping sauce 93
   watercress salad with roasted capsicum, lentils and haloumi 110
carbohydrates 10, 12, 19
cardiovascular disease 13, 15, 17
carrots 15, 17
   black bean chilli on soft polenta 225
   carrot, beetroot and mint salad 130
   carrot and quinoa cupcakes with tofu cashew 'cream' 153
   coconut chapati, bean and salad stacks 89
   fresh spring rolls 90
   green goddess slaw with chickpeas 114
   julienned summer veggie salad 133
   lentil Bolognese 221
   lentil shepherd's pies 226
   okonomiyaki (Japanese pancake) 84
   quick minestrone 176
   roasted with garlic and dukkah 235
   socca with roasted carrots, feta and seeds 196
   stir fried veggies with honey, soy and basil tofu 140
   summertime rice paper rolls with peanut dipping sauce 93
   vegetable koftas with tomato and tamarind sauce 143
cashews
   cauliflower and cashew korma curry 205
   lentil and cashew burgers 181
   tofu cashew 'cream' 153
cauliflower 15, 17, 20
   cauliflower and cashew korma curry 205
   pizza 195
chicken 20
chickpeas 13, 19, 20, 22, 34–5, 39
   apple cake 245
   baked eggplant with chickpeas and green chilli 222

basil-pesto hommus 69
chickpea and lentil burgers with avocado salsa 83
chickpea crepes 216
cooking 35, 43
desi 35
dried 35
Greek salad with avocado and chickpeas 113
green goddess slaw with chickpeas 114
heavenly hommus 69
kabuli 35
Moroccan hommus 69
my favourite falafels 186
nutrient composition 24
peanut butter chickpea energy balls 154
pumpkin and chickpea curry 202
quick minestrone 176
roasted capsicum hommus 69
salads 65, 107
semi-dried tomato and basil hommus 69
spiced-up hommus 69
sprouting 53–5
tinned 35
chicory root 13
chilli
   baked eggplant with chickpeas and green chilli 222
   chilli and cinnamon roasted Brussels sprouts 236
   muhumarra 73
chives 17
chocolate
   black bean brownie 246
   mousse 149
cholesterol 12, 17, 22
chunky monkey ice cream 150
climate change 10
coconut
   coconut chapati, bean and salad stacks 89
   sesame coconut ice cream 150
coleslaw
   green goddess slaw with chickpeas 114
   kale slaw 129
conversion charts 268
corn 12, 13, 19, 25, 57
   barley and corn salad with miso dressing 120
   black bean salad with corn and avocado 103

tomatoey eggplant and lentils on sweetcorn polenta 144
cornmeal *see* polenta
crackers, seedy 250
creamy cannellini bean and kale soup 175
creamy potato salad with butter beans and mint 104
crêpes
   chickpea 216
   fresh spring rolls 90
cucumber
   Greek salad with avocado and chickpeas 113
   sprouted spring salad 134
   summertime rice paper rolls with peanut dipping sauce 93
cupcakes, carrot and quinoa with tofu cashew 'cream' 153
curries 167, 199
   cauliflower and cashew korma 205
   green curry with tofu 206
   pumpkin and chickpea 202
   quick lentil 201

D

dairy 25
desserts 65, 147, 167, 239 *see also* sweets
   baked apples with seedy nutty topping 241
   banana 'caramel' ice cream 150
   banana choc chip ice cream 150
   banana ice cream 150
   chocolate mousse 149
   chunky monkey ice cream 150
   lemon mousse 149
   mango mousse 149
   mixed berry gelato 150
   raspberry mousse 149
   rhubarb and walnut crumble 242
   sesame coconut ice cream 150
DHA (docosahexaenoic acid) 20
diabetes 12, 15, 17, 19, 22
dips 65, 67
   basil-pesto hommus 69
   beetroot dip 70
   dukkah 249
   heavenly hommus 69
   Moroccan hommus 69
   muhumarra 73
   roasted capsicum hommus 69
   semi-dried tomato and basil hommus 69
   spiced-up hommus 69
   white bean aioli 74

white bean and basil 74
white bean with garlic and herbs 74
DPA (docosapentaenoic acid) 20
dressings 59
   barley salad with basil 119
   black bean salad 103
   black Beluga lentil salad 232
   brown rice salad 124
   carrot and beetroot salad 130
   green goddess 114
   julienned summer veggie salad 133
   miso 120
   sprouted spring salad 134
   watercress salad 110
dukkah 249
   carrots roasted with garlic and dukkah 235
dysbiosis 13

E
edamame 39
   kale, quinoa, edamame and avocado salad 129
eggplant 17
   baked eggplant with chickpeas and green chilli 222
   eggplant and adzuki bean burgers 80
   eggplant with yoghurt and coriander 212
   lentil Bolognese 221
   quick lentil curry 201
   tomatoey eggplant and lentils on sweetcorn polenta 144
eggs 20, 25
   vegan egg replacer 250
enchiladas, black bean with kale and guacamole 191
endives 13
energy balls, peanut butter chickpea 154
EPA (eicosapentaenoic acid) 20
extra virgin olive oil (EVOO) 58

F
falafels 186
fats 10, 12, 20
   omega 3 20
fava beans 39
feta
   barley salad with tomatoes, feta and basil 119
   beetroot, lentil, feta and walnut salad 109
   Greek salad with avocado and chickpeas 113
   socca with roasted carrots, feta and seeds 196
fibre 10, 12–13, 15
   gut microbiome, and 13
   insoluble 12
   resistant starch 12
   soluble 12
   what is 12
fish 20
free radicals 14
freekeh 47
   cooking 47
fresh spring rolls 90
fruit 12, 14, 16
   colour groups 15, 17
   daily servings 16
   seasonal food guide 62, 63, 164, 165
   skins 16

G
garlic 13, 15, 17
   black-eyed peas with garlic and lemon 100
   carrots roasted with garlic and dukkah 235
   white bean dip with garlic and herbs 74
Glycaemic Index (GI) 19, 25
   salads, and 57
grains *see also by name*
   cooking with 47–8
   daily servings 16
   salads 65, 117
   sprouting 53–5
   whole *see* whole grains
grapefruit 17
grapes 17
Greek salad with avocado and chickpeas 113
green beans
   okonomiyaki (Japanese pancake) 84
   quick lentil curry 201
green curry with tofu 206
green goddess slaw with chickpeas 114
greenhouse gas emissions (GHG) 10
greens, leafy 17

H
haloumi, watercress salad with roasted capsicum, lentils and 110
healthy food 9
heart disease 12, 20, 22
heavenly hommus 69
herbs
   fresh 59
   seasonal food guide 62, 63, 164, 165
honey 13
   stir fried veggies with honey, soy and basil tofu 140

I
Indian food 167, 209–17
   curries *see* curries
indoles 17
inflammation 12, 13, 14, 20
insoluble fibre 12
insulin 19
irritable bowel syndrome (IBS) 13

J
julienned summer veggie salad 133

K
kale 17, 20, 22
   black bean enchiladas with kale and guacamole 191
   black Beluga lentil salad with baby kale, pumpkin and beetroot 232
   creamy cannellini bean and kale soup 175
   kale, quinoa and almond salad 129
   kale, quinoa, edamame and avocado salad 129
   nutrient composition 24
   slaw 129
   super simple kale salad (with variations) 129
kidney beans 20, 24, 38, 39
   cooking 38, 43
   mushroom and bean burgers 182
   quick minestrone 176
   super-speedy kidney bean wraps 192
kimchi 13
kiwifruit 17
koftas with tomato and tamarind sauce 143

L
'leaky gut' 13
leeks 13, 17
   pumpkin, leek and red lentil soup 171
legumes 10, 12, 13, 14, 16, 19, 20, 25, 27–9
   cooking guide 43
   daily servings 16
   mains 137
   salads 57
   types and uses 39

lemons 17
   black-eyed peas with garlic and lemon 100
   lemony lentil soup 172
   mousse 149
lentils 13, 19, 22, 31–2, 39
   beetroot, lentil, feta and walnut salad 109
   black Beluga 32
   black Beluga salad with baby kale, pumpkin and beetroot 232
   Bolognese 221
   brown/green 31, 32
   chickpea and lentil burgers with avocado salsa 83
   cooking 31–2, 43
   French green 31
   lemony lentil soup 172
   lentil and cashew burgers 181
   nutrient composition 24
   pumpkin, leek and red lentil soup 171
   Puy 31, 32
   quick lentil curry 201
   quinoa, lentil and broccoli salad 123
   red 31, 32
   red lentil dhal 215
   salads 65, 107
   shepherd's pies 226
   sprouted spring salad 134
   sprouting 53–5
   tomatoey eggplant and lentils on sweetcorn polenta 144
   types 31
   watercress salad with roasted capsicum, lentils and haloumi 110
lettuce 17
Lima (butter) beans 24, 38, 39
   cooking 38, 43
   creamy potato salad with butter beans and mint 104
   white bean aioli 74
   white bean and basil dip 74
   white bean dip with garlic and herbs 74
linseeds 20
lutein 17
lycopene 17

M

macular degeneration 15, 17
mains, seasonal 65, 167, 219
mango 17
   black bean and mango salad 103
   mousse 149

marinated bean salad 99
meal planning 262–5
meat 10
metabolic syndrome 13
millet 48, 54
   cooking 48
minerals 10, 15, 25
mint
   creamy potato salad with butter beans and mint 104
miso 13
   dressing 120
mixed berry gelato 150
Moroccan hommus 69
muesli 19
muhumarra 73
mung beans 40, 54
   cooking 40, 43
mushrooms 22
   black bean chilli on soft polenta 225
   lentil Bolognese 221
   lentil shepherd's pies 226
   mushroom and bean burgers 182
   stir fried veggies with honey, soy and basil tofu 140
my favourite falafels 186

N

nutritional information 266
nuts 12, 14, 19, 20, 22, 25 *see also by name*
   dukkah 249
   sprouting 53–5

O

oats 12, 13, 19, 48
   cooking 48
   nutrient composition 24
obesity 13, 14
okonomiyaki (Japanese pancake) 84
olive oil 58
olives
   Greek salad with avocado and chickpeas 113
onions 13, 15, 17
oranges 17

P

paneer ka salan 211
pantry staples 260
parsnip 13, 19
pasta 12, 19
   lentil Bolognese 221
   raw tomato sauce with zoodles 139
   wholemeal 25

peaches 17
peanut butter chickpea energy balls 154
peanut dipping sauce 93
pear 17
peas 13, 17, 19
   black-eyed see black-eyed peas
   split see split peas
pesto 253
phenolics 17
phytonutrients 10, 15–16, 25
pizzas 167, 189
   cauliflower 195
   socca with roasted carrots, feta and seeds 196
plant-based intake 9
   benefits 10
   foods 12
   how to increase your 25
   nutrient composition table 24
   protein, and 22
plums 17
polenta 13, 47
   black bean chilli on soft polenta 225
   cooking 47
   tomatoey eggplant and lentils on sweetcorn polenta 144
pomegranate molasses 253
potatoes 12, 19, 25, 57
   creamy potato salad with butter beans and mint 104
prebiotics 13
probiotics 13
processed foods 10, 19
protein 10, 12, 21–2, 25
   guide to plant-based 256–8
   'protein combining' 22
prunes 17
pumpkin 17, 19
   black Beluga lentil salad with baby kale, pumpkin and beetroot 232
   cauliflower pizza 195
   pumpkin and chickpea curry 202
   pumpkin, leek and red lentil soup 171
   pumpkin, semi-dried tomato and tofu burgers 185
   quick lentil curry 201
   quick minestrone 176
pumpkin seeds 24

Q

quick lentil curry 201
quick minestrone soup 176
quinoa 25, 48, 54
   black bean and quinoa burgers 79

carrot and quinoa cupcakes with tofu cashew 'cream' 153
cooking 48
kale, quinoa and almond salad 129
kale, quinoa, edamame and avocado salad 129
nutrient composition 24
quinoa and brown rice California rolls 94
quinoa, lentil and broccoli salad 123

R

radishes 54
   julienned summer veggie salad 133
   sprouted spring salad 134
raisins 17
raspberries 17
   coulis 246
   mixed berry gelato 150
   mousse 149
raw tomato sauce with zoodles 139
red lentil dhal 215
refried beans
   coconut chapati, bean and salad stacks 89
resistant starch 12
rhubarb and walnut crumble 242
rice 12, 47
   brown 25, 47
   brown rice salad 124
   cooking 47
   quinoa and brown rice California rolls 94
   wild 47, 54
roasted capsicum hommus 69
roasted vegetable and barley salad 231
rye 13

S

salads 25, 57–9, 229
   bean 97 *see also by type of bean*
   chickpea *see* chickpeas
   dressings *see* dressings
   grain 117 *see also by type of grain*
   how to make great 59
   lentil 107 *see also by type of lentil*
   marinated bean salad 99
   roasted vegetable and barley 231
   seasonal 65, 167
   vegetable 127 *see also by name of vegetable*
salsa, avocado 83
salt 256
sauces
   peanut dipping 93

quick tomato relish 254
raspberry coulis 246
raw tomato 139
stir fried veggies 140
tahini 186
tomato and tamarind 143
sauerkraut 13
seasonal foods 9, 61–3, 163–5
   recipes 65, 167
seeds 12, 14, 19, 20, 22, 25
   baked apples with seedy nutty topping 241
   seedy crackers 250
   socca with roasted carrots, feta and seeds 196
   sprouting 53–5
semi-dried tomato and basil hommus 69
sesame coconut ice cream 150
short-chain fatty acids (SCFAs) 12
side dishes
   carrots roasted with garlic and dukkah 235
   chilli and cinnamon roasted Brussels sprouts 236
   seasonal 167, 229
snow peas
   fresh spring rolls 90
   julienned summer veggie salad 133
socca with roasted carrots, feta and seeds 196
soluble fibre 12
soups 167, 169
   creamy cannellini bean and kale 175
   lemony lentil 172
   pumpkin, leek and red lentil 171
   quick minestrone 176
soy beans 13, 20, 22, 40
   cooking 40
   nutrient composition 24
   stir fried veggies with honey, soy and basil tofu 140
spelt 48
   cooking 48
spiced-up hommus 69
spinach 17
   coconut chapati, bean and salad stacks 89
split peas 22, 24, 33
   cooking 33, 43
spring
   meal planner 264
   plant-based protein guide 256
   recipes 65
   seasonal food guide 61, 62

spring onions 17
   stir fried veggies with honey, soy and basil tofu 140
spring rolls, fresh 90
sprouted spring salad 134
sprouting 53–5
   benefits 53
   containers 55
   guidelines 54–5
   troubleshooting 55
   using sprouts 54
   when to sprout 54
stacks 65, 87
   coconut chapati, bean and salad 89
   stir fried veggies with honey, soy and basil tofu 140
strawberries 17
sumac 254
summer
   meal planner 264
   plant-based protein guide 256
   recipes 65
   seasonal food guide 61, 63
summertime rice paper rolls with peanut dipping sauce 93
sunflower seeds 54
super simple kale salad 129
super-speedy kidney bean wraps 192
sweet potato 17, 19, 57
   lentil shepherd's pies 226
   nutrient composition 24
sweets 65, 147, 167, 239 *see also* desserts
   apple cake 245
   black bean brownie 246
   carrot and quinoa cupcakes with tofu cashew 'cream' 153
   peanut butter chickpea energy balls 154

T

tamari 254
tamarind purée 254
tofu 20, 22, 25, 45
   baked 45
   chocolate mousse 149
   cooking with 45
   fresh spring rolls 90
   green curry with tofu 206
   lemon mousse 149
   mango mousse 149
   nutrient composition 24
   pan-fried 45
   pumpkin, semi-dried tomato and tofu burgers 185
   raspberry mousse 149

stir fried veggies with honey, soy and basil tofu 140
tofu cashew 'cream' 153
tomatoes 17
    barley salad with tomatoes, feta and basil 119
    black bean chilli on soft polenta 225
    coconut chapati, bean and salad stacks 89
    Greek salad with avocado and chickpeas 113
    julienned summer veggie salad 133
    marinated bean salad 99
    pumpkin, semi-dried tomato and tofu burgers 185
    quick minestrone 176
    quick tomato relish 254
    raw tomato sauce with zoodles 139
    semi-dried tomato and basil hommus 69
    super-speedy kidney bean wraps 192
    tomato and tamarind sauce 143
    tomatoey eggplant and lentils on sweetcorn polenta 144
turmeric 254

V

vegetable oils 20
vegetables 10, 12, 14, 16, 25
    colour groups 15, 17
    cooking 16, 161
    daily servings 16
    koftas with tomato and tamarind sauce 143
    mains 137
    roasted vegetable and barley salad 231
    roasting 161
    salads 65, 127
    seasonal food guide 62, 63, 164, 165
    skins 16
    vegetable stock paste 255
vegetarian diet 9, 10
vitamins 10, 14, 15, 25, 163

W

walnuts 20
    beetroot, lentil, feta and walnut salad 109
    muhumarra 73
    rhubarb and walnut crumble 242
watercress 17
    salad with roasted capsicum, lentils and haloumi 110
    sprouted spring salad 134
weight management 12, 14
wheat 13
    cooking 48
wheat berries 54
white beans *see* cannellini beans; Lima (butter) beans
whole grains 10, 12, 14, 16, 20, 22, 25
    cooking with 47–8
    daily servings 16
winter
    meal planner 265
    plant-based protein guide 258
    recipes 167
    seasonal food guide 163, 165
wraps 65, 87, 167, 189
    black bean enchiladas with kale and guacamole 191
    fresh spring rolls 90
    quinoa and brown rice California rolls 94
    summertime rice paper rolls with peanut dipping sauce 93
    super-speedy kidney bean wraps 192

Y

yams 19
yoghurt 13
    eggplant with yoghurt and coriander 212

Z

zucchini
    black bean chilli on soft polenta 225
    cauliflower pizza 195
    fresh spring rolls 90
    green curry with tofu 206
    julienned summer veggie salad 133
    lentil shepherd's pies 226
    okonomiyaki (Japanese pancake) 84
    raw tomato sauce with zoodles 139

Veggie-licious

First published as two eBooks in 2016 by Caroline Trickey
© Caroline Trickey 2016
This edition © Caroline Trickey 2017

All rights reserved. No part of this book may be reproduced, stored in a retrieval system, or transmitted in any form or by any means, electronic, electrostatic, magnetic tape, mechanical, photocopying, recording or otherwise, without permission in writing from the publisher.

A catalogue record of this book is available from the National Library of Australia

ISBN: 978-0-6481700-0-6

Text, recipes and photographs © Caroline Trickey
Food styling assistance: Cydne Flatter and Deborah Phillips
Additional photographs: Author photograph Kate Williams Photography; page 152 Arnaldo Aldana, Unsplash; page 252 Artur Rutkowski, Unsplash
Proofreading and index: Puddingburn
Design: Avril Makula

Thank you to Catherine Saxelby whose ongoing guidance and advice has been invaluable. Enormous gratitude to the talented Avril who has made my words look amazing in print and been so kind and patient to the still very novice author! I am indebted to my wonderful husband's generosity and patience. It is amazing to have someone so kind and considerate who believes in me. Thanks also to my fabulous proofreaders Ashton, Catherine, Deborah and Avril.

www.healthyhomecafe.com

www.ingramcontent.com/pod-product-compliance
Lightning Source LLC
Chambersburg PA
CBHW042146290426
44110CB00003B/132